Financial Planning—
The Next Step

A Practical Approach to Merging Your Clients' Money with Their Lives

Roy T. Diliberto, CFP®

The Financial Planning Association (FPA) is the membership association for the financial planning community. FPA is committed to providing information and resources to help financial planners and those who champion the financial planning process succeed. FPA believes that everyone needs objective advice to make smart financial decisions.

FPA Press is the publishing arm of FPA, providing current content and advanced thinking on technical and practice management topics.

Information in this book is accurate at the time of publication and consistent with the standards of good practice in the financial planning community. As research and practice advance, however, standards may change. For this reason, it is recommended that readers evaluate the applicability of any recommendation in light of particular situations and changing standards.

Disclaimer—This publication is designed to provide accurate and authoritative information in regard to the subject matter covered. It is sold with the understanding that the publisher is not engaged in rendering legal, accounting, or other professional service. If legal advice or other expert assistance is required, the services of a competent professional person should be sought. —*From a Declaration of Principles jointly adopted by a Committee of the American Bar Association and a Committee of Publishers and Associations.*

The views or opinions expressed by the author are the responsibility of the author alone and do not imply a view or opinion on the part of FPA, its members, employees, or agents. No representation or warranty is made concerning the accuracy of the material presented nor the application of the principles discussed by the author to any specific fact situation. The proper interpretation or application of the principles discussed in this FPA Publication is a matter of considered judgment of the person using the FPA Publication and FPA disclaims all liability therefore.

No part of this publication may be reproduced, stored in a retrieval system, or transmitted in any form or by any means, electronic, mechanical, photocopying, recording, or otherwise, without prior written permission of the publisher.

The Financial Planning Association is the owner of trademark, service mark, and collective membership mark rights in FPA®, FPA/Logo and FINANCIAL PLANNING ASSOCIATION®. The marks may not be used without written permission from the Financial Planning Association.

CFP®, CERTIFIED FINANCIAL PLANNER™, and federally registered CFP (with flame logo) are certification marks owned by Certified Financial Planner Board of Standards. These marks are awarded to individuals who successfully complete CFP Board's initial and ongoing certification requirements.

Financial Planning Association
4100 Mississippi Ave., Suite 400
Denver, Colorado 80246-3053

Phone: 800.322.4237
Fax: 303.759-0749
E-mail: fpapress@fpanet.org

www.fpanet.org

Copyright © 2006 FPA Press. All rights reserved.

ISBN: 0-9753448-4-6
ISBN-13 978-09753448-4-2

Manufactured in the United States of America

Financial Planning— The Next Step

A Practical Approach to Merging Your Clients' Money with Their Lives

*To my wife and life partner, Peggy,
who has been a part of my life and
my inspiration for 19 years.*

About the Author

Roy Diliberto, CFP®, is founder and Chief Executive Officer of RTD Financial Advisors, Inc., a comprehensive financial life planning firm with offices in Philadelphia and West Chester, Pennsylvania; Mount Laurel, New Jersey; and Bonita Springs, Florida. A graduate of Temple University, Diliberto received his Chartered Financial Consultant designation from the American College and his Certified Financial Planner designation from the College for Financial Planning.

Roy has been quoted in many national and local publications including *The Wall Street Journal, The New York Times, Philadelphia Magazine, The Philadelphia Inquirer, USA Today, The Boston Globe, The Washington Post*, and *The L.A. Times*. He has been named as one of the best financial planners in America by several publications, including *Money, Worth*, and *Medical Economics*. *Investment Advisor* magazine identified him as "One of the 25 Most Influential People in the Financial Planning Profession," and *Financial Planning* magazine recently named him to the "Movers and Shakers" hall of fame. He has appeared on national television programs such as *The NBC Nightly News with Tom Brokaw, CNN Moneytalk, Fox on Money, Up to the Minute* on CBS, and *Business Center* on CNBC. He has also been featured on ABCNEWS.COM and CNNFN.

Active in professional and civic associations, Roy served as the first national president of the Financial Planning Association. He was on the advisory boards of Schwab Institutional and TD Waterhouse. He is a member of the Temple University Planned Giving Advisory Council and the Temple Owl Club Board of Directors. He also writes a bimonthly column on Financial Life Planning for *Financial Advisor* magazine, and is a frequent speaker at industry meetings.

Roy is considered one of the profession's most passionate proponents of financial life planning. He brings this passion to his practice by helping his clients pursue their goals and dreams.

Roy is donating his royalties from this book to the Foundation for Financial Planning.

Acknowledgements

I would like to thank the many people who have helped me directly and indirectly in the writing of this book. The advisers who were willing to share their methodologies and client stories with me: Harv Ames, Bob Barry, Janet Briaud, Elissa Buie, Grady Cash, Gayle Colman, Rich Colman, A.J. Diliberto, Jon Guyton, Elizabeth Jetton, Rick Kahler, Ross Levin, Michael Smith, Lewis Walker, and Marcee Yager. To the mentor in my life, who inspired me to do the right thing: Vince Bowhers. To George Kinder, who helped me to discover myself and provided tools that I use in helping clients discover who they are. To Mitch Anthony, who supplied me with a missing link in my practice—a transferable system for client discovery and ongoing service. He also gave me the confidence to begin this project.

And to Rich Busillo and Jeff Weiand, without whom our firm could have never grown to be successful.

About FPA

The Financial Planning Association® (FPA®) is the membership organization for the financial planning community. FPA is built around four Core Values—Competence, Integrity, Relationships, and Stewardship. We want as members those who share our Core Values.

FPA's primary aim is to be the community that fosters the value of financial planning and advances the financial planning profession. The FPA strategy to accomplish its objectives involves welcoming all those who advance the financial planning process and promoting the CERTIFIED FINANCIAL PLANNER™ (CFP®) marks as the cornerstone of the financial planning profession. FPA is the heart of financial planning, connecting those who deliver, support, and benefit from it.

FPA was created on the foundation that the CFP marks best represent the promise and the future of the financial planning profession. CFP certification offers the public a consistent and credible symbol of professional competence in financial planning. And FPA benefits the public by helping to ensure that financial planning is delivered through competent and ethical financial planners.

FPA members include individuals and companies who are dedicated to helping people make wise financial decisions to achieve their life goals and dreams. FPA believes that everyone needs objective advice to make smart financial decisions and that when seeking the advice of a financial planner, the planner should be a CFP professional.

FPA is committed to improving and enhancing the professional lives and capabilities of our members. We offer a variety of programs and services to that end.

Table of Contents

Preface

I used to tell people that the so-called "life planning" movement in the financial planning profession finally came of age when Roy Diliberto publicly embraced it.

There were actually two reasons why I believed this to be true. First, and most obviously, Roy was on track to become president of the new FPA, and he used that pulpit to openly declare, to highly skeptical audiences, that the profession needed to move in a new and better direction, to embrace a more personal and ultimately more useful service standard for its clients. It was a rare example of an organization that got ahead of an innovation instead of resisting it until it had become a *fait accompli*.

And in his speeches, Roy phrased the debate in a way that made it hard to take the opposite position. He would ask a question that the skeptics had no answer for: what was the point of applying technical skills to a person's situation when you had an incomplete understanding of that situation?

But the more important reason why his embrace of life planning was so important was that Roy was, in temperament and personal history, one of the skeptics himself. He was known as a hard-nosed technician who did not chase down every fad; he had credibility among the advisers who believed that any newfangled innovation had to prove itself before they would put it to work in their practices.

Thus, when Roy embraced this new and rather complicated service standard, it was clear that he had put it through its paces. Unlike the quasi-social workers and idealists who jumped on the life planning bandwagon from inception, he demanded that life planning prove its worth in the practical arena, that it benefit the client relationship in demonstrable ways.

Of course, I was also a proponent of the service innovations, and in my newsletter, in speeches, and in my magazine columns, I would make what I thought were terrifically well-organized arguments in their favor. It was a little humbling to notice that I didn't get much traction with the most successful segment of the profession until one of *them*, a respected technician like Roy Diliberto, came out in favor of asking George Kinder's three famous questions as a routine part of the client engagement. It gave the whole concept a new credibility.

That was a turning point. From that moment on, nobody could ask, with a straight face, whether there was any real-world benefit to what was then derided as "this touchy-feely stuff." The touchy-feely stuff must have a real-world benefit or somebody like Roy would have dismissed it with good-natured contempt.

What *is* life planning? We now realize that it is simply a better way to do financial planning. In the early days, when new innovations and better questions and service ideas came out monthly, it seemed like life planning was something new, perhaps bigger than financial planning itself. What we didn't realize at the time was that it was just like every innovation in a profession; life planning did nothing more—or less—than become a new and important part of financial planning and make it better, in the same way that managing client assets and keeping accurate track of yearly performance had made the planning service better a decade ago. (We thought that was a revolution too.)

Life planning is asking better questions at the beginning of the engagement, it is listening better to the answers, it is applying the planning toolbox to help clients achieve personal as well as objective goals, and it is caring more for the well-being of clients. It is financial planning, but the people who incorporated life planning tools were setting it on a much more secure and powerful foundation than anybody had done before.

Of course, all of these things are far more easily said than done, just as it is easy to say that a certain client situation calls for the creation of a charitable remainder unitrust with catchup provisions as a supplement to a client's retirement income planning. The devil is always in the details.

This book you hold in your hands is a compendium of practical details, a guide, if you will, to the way the new service can be applied in the real world. I can tell you from personal (and sometimes contentious, sometimes affectionate) experience that the author of this book is not and never has been interested in theories that have no useful application.

That, I think, is what makes this book so different from what I've read before on the subject of what we must now start calling "better financial planning." You will not waste a moment listening to sermons here. If you are still among the unconverted, then your belief in adding life planning to your practice will have to come from practical applications and client stories—and, occasionally, inspirational stories about other professions. (What surprisingly powerful lessons can you learn from a successful home builder? Or about the service guy employed by a retailer of recreational boats?)

My guess is that after you finish, you will find yourself making a lot of small adjustments as well as the big ones that you're looking for. You'll get some real-world examples on how estate and philanthropic planning can move beyond the technical aspects to enhance the client experience and deepen the client relationship. Instead of being told that customer service is important, you'll get a mini-spreadsheet on the tangible financial benefits of excellent customer service. You'll get a practical discussion of the importance of teamwork and a practical guide to creating and compensating a functional team. The tour includes a look at the frontier of fees, and a reminder of something that all of us forget: how to take care of yourself as you tend your business.

I hope that you, the reader, are still a skeptic, because I believe in the life planning component of "better financial planning," and I think it will take nothing less than the lessons and observations of this book to convince you at this late date.

More likely, you know that the service is important, you have been offering a version of it for years, and now you want to do it better.

Either way, you'll get the benefit of a lot of good thinking, by a person who has had to defend, and defend well, a new way of doing business even as he was pioneering its most practical aspects. I have debated Roy on many occasions in the past, and we have agreed and disagreed on many things, and I expect all that to continue. One thing we agree on is that this book is a pretty good way to get from traditional financial planning to better financial planning in a hurry, without any wasted energy, and with good insight and wisdom. What more could you ask for from a professional book?

—*Bob Veres*
May 2006

Introduction

*That man pursues a great variety of goals,
but the one he seeks as his ultimate end is happiness.
Everything else is a means not an end.*

—Socrates

It was early on September 11, 2001, when I awoke in my hotel room in San Diego (I had arrived the night before and was still functioning on East Coast time). The Financial Planning Association's (FPA) Annual Conference was scheduled to begin that evening. As I was preparing for a day of Board meetings, I turned on the news to see the horrors of the day. When I understood that America was being attacked and that airplanes were being used as weapons, my thoughts immediately went to my son, A.J., and his family. He was flying from Philadelphia to Los Angeles with his wife and three children. Nothing mattered to me until I knew they were safe (they got as far as Chicago before all flights were cancelled).

That day changed the lives and priorities of most of us. Mitch Anthony, founder of The Financial Life

Planning Institute, tells the story of a financial planner who told him, "Yesterday, we worked with our clients' assets; today, we work with their hearts." This is *the* profound shift that will determine whether people begin to use their assets to create a life that will give them the meaning and satisfaction they crave. Tragedies such as 9/11 cause us to re-examine our goals and priorities in life. When I sat in that hotel room, I thought of my son, my daughter-in-law, and my grandchildren—not my portfolio or my practice. It is our job as financial planners to help our clients discover—or re-discover—what is most important in their lives and help them to plan accordingly. We can truly make a difference in the lives of our clients, perhaps more than any other professionals can. *If not us, then who else?*

One of my clients had a life-altering experience after 9/11. Here are her words: "I was a senior vice president at a large upscale fashion designer and lost a family member on 9/11. Life was never the same again. I realized I didn't want to be doing what I had been doing—for the money, for the things. I wanted to be giving to others in a very personal and individual way. My friends were shocked that I would walk away from the life I had, but I haven't missed it for a minute. It took me a long time to come to what I'm passionate about, but I've never been happier." Rather than point out the financial difficulties of this dramatic change, we helped her to achieve her goal of becoming a massage therapist and t'ai chi chih teacher.

Shortly after 9/11, I got a call from a client, a widow who was 70 years old. While she had enough money to last her lifetime, she did not have so much that she could afford to be frivolous or irresponsible. She recounted a dream she and her husband had to take their two children and four grandchildren on a vacation throughout Europe. However, they always seemed to find some reason for putting it off. After her husband's death, her fear of running out of money resulted in her putting the goal on hold indefinitely. But 9/11 changed that. She became more sensitive to the uncertainly of the future and developed a keen awareness of her need to be with her family. She told me that spending less in the future, if she had to, would be a small tradeoff for this family time that she so desperately wanted and needed. While this trip was to cost about $50,000, the price for not doing it was much higher than she was willing to pay. My experience since 9/11 is that many people who were obsessed with saving money for the future have reassessed their goals and are craving a balance between enjoying life today and ensuring their future security. I try to help them find it. If that is "life planning," then I am guilty of practicing it.

Following a presentation on life planning made at Success Forum 2002 in New Orleans, Rich Rojeck, a past Chair of IAFP, asked a cogent question: "Do we need to label what we are doing as 'life planning,' or is it just *financial planning done well?*" I have always objected to the term "life planning" because, in my opinion, it does not accurately describe what we do or what most of us have been trained to do. Ask the average person what a life planner does, and you are not likely to hear, "financial planning that takes into consideration my life issues and attitudes about money before giving advice." Yet that is how I would define this "movement" that some people in our profession insist on labeling life planning. Dick Wagner, who practices in Denver, calls it "integral finance," others say they are dealing with their clients' "interior" issues, and Mitch Anthony has coined the phrase "financial life planning." It matters little to me what the brand is, but for our purposes in this book, we will refer to the process as "financial life planning."

In my opinion, merging our clients' money with their lives (financial life planning) is simply the next logical step in the development of our profession. I have always believed that financial planning advice is goal-oriented, but my processes have not always been successful in uncovering what was really important to my clients. When I first started practicing financial planning over 20 years ago, I used a "fact-finder." It contained mostly quantitative questions to determine how much they owned, how much they spent, how much they paid in taxes, how much insurance they had, how much return they wanted on their money, etc. The section on goals was very brief. It listed typical goals that many people have, such as retiring at a certain age, providing for children's educations, family security in the event of death or disability, saving income taxes, estate planning, etc. They were asked to number each in its order of priority. We put a dollar value on these goals, determined what they had to do to reach their objectives, and made our recommendations. Several years later, the questions became more open-ended and actually gave them opportunities to have some goals that were not listed. The results were somewhat better, but far from ideal. Now we probe our clients' histories, values, goals, and attitudes about money. The first two client meetings (approximately two hours each) are devoted to this discovery process. We do not discuss quantitative issues at these meetings unless there is a pressing concern that needs to be dealt with immediately.

The point I am making is that, in 1983, we were practicing *financial planning*, and 22 years later, we are still practicing *financial planning*. We just got better at it. The processes outlined in this book are compilations of tools we got from

George Kinder, Mitch Anthony, other planners, and ourselves. It is dynamic and we are always looking for ways to improve it.

But are we "crossing the line" between practicing financial planning and practicing psychology? When speaking to financial planners about using a more thorough discovery process, some of them have expressed this concern. While I certainly acknowledge that what we are doing might have a psychological component (how do we interact with another human being in ways that do not?), it is not the practice of psychology, because we do not offer therapy. Just about every planner I know asks clients about their risk tolerance. What is that, if not psychological? However, I do share some of their concerns. Financial planners should be careful not to attempt to "treat" serious problems such as addictive spending, hoarding, spousal conflict, unreasonable fear, etc. I am neither qualified nor licensed to practice in these areas. We certainly would not expect psychologists who uncover financial problems with their patients to give financial planning advice. And financial planners who discover serious money issues should refer these clients to other professionals. Just as you would not draw a will for a client (unless you are an attorney), you should not attempt to go beyond your areas of expertise. As a CFP practitioner, I am bound by the CFP Board's Code of Ethics, which says, "A CFP designee shall offer advice only in those areas in which the CFP designee has competence."[1] However, I do believe it is our obligation as holistic financial planners to help our clients uncover any constraints they may have about money, to understand their core values, and to discover the most important goals and dreams in their lives. *The value of our advice will improve in proportion to the knowledge we have about our clients.*

While it is true that many people have changed their behaviors as a result of the work we do (this book will be full of stories[2] that demonstrate that), they did it on their own after the discovery process and their own realizations that they could accomplish their goals and live less stressful lives by concentrating on what was important to them. Therefore, this book will not provide any advice on how to cure your clients' psychological ills. It will show you how to put into practice a discovery and implementation process that will help you to merge your clients' money with their lives.

I am indebted to many people who have helped me on this journey. When I attended George Kinder's workshop, "The Seven Stages of Money Maturity," I discovered the origins behind much of my behavior around money and what goals really mattered in my life. His insights have not only improved my life, but my clients' lives as well. Dick Wagner, in his writings on integral finance, has opened a rich dialogue among financial planners that has improved my approach to financial planning. Mitch Anthony provided materials for me that helped to make the process of financial life planning consistent and transferable to others.

In the chapters that follow, you will learn how to travel the journey with your clients from the initial consultation to the planning process to ongoing service. We will discuss how to organize your firm, charge for your services, compensate your staff, and get everyone in your firm on the same page. It is the practical approach to merging your clients' money with their lives.

ENDNOTES
1. CFP Code of Ethics, Rule 301
2. Names and some circumstances have been changed to protect identities.

1

Getting Started: Who is Your Client?

If you don't understand yourself you don't understand anybody else.

—Nikki Giovanni, poet

MONEY MANAGER OR FINANCIAL LIFE PLANNER

Several years ago, I attended a FPA symposium in Minneapolis and one of the speakers was George Kinder, often called the "father of life planning." To demonstrate his process for planning, he discussed a client with whom he had recently worked. She was a woman who had come into a large sum of money and was feeling frozen and desperate for answers. This newfound wealth, and the responsibility she believed went with it, was causing her to experience anxiety. She was not comfortable spending it on luxuries for herself, and investing it just to increase its value seemed selfish, if not mercenary. George shared how, over several meetings, he coached her through a process that helped her to articulate and prioritize specific goals for her life.

He showed her how she could use the money to help others (a goal that was very important to her). She began to feel comfortable with her wealth and, eventually, her desperation was converted to joy and satisfaction.

After George's session, we adjourned to lunch where the speaker was a money manager. He began by asking for a show of hands of who among us would feel desperate if given $5 million. He shook his head, looked down at the podium, and proclaimed, "I guess I just don't get it." Of course, he didn't "get it." Asking him to understand George and his work would have been like convincing a surgeon that holistic medicine is the wave of the future. Everything in his training and background taught him that growing the money is the only goal that matters and everything else will take care of itself. He probably believes that money really could buy happiness. The fact that it could actually cause someone to feel anything but euphoria confused him. If that woman had walked into his office, he, no doubt, would have begun the discussion with charts, graphs, and statistics. He probably would have demonstrated that value investing is superior to all other styles in the long run. And he would have deluded himself into believing that this woman was actually his client. However, he would have been mistaken. His client is the money. Moreover, he is not alone. After all, they do call themselves *money* managers. It's not that I believe that money managers do not perform valuable functions, because they do. However, we should not confuse them with financial life planners, whose focus is on their clients and their unique goals, dreams, values, and aspirations. Growing money may be one way to help them achieve some of these goals, but it certainly is not the only way.

Financial life planners show clients how they can use money to enhance their lives. They never lose sight of the fact that money is a means to an end—a wonderful servant, but a poor master. They understand that spending money, not growing it, may be appropriate for many clients. And they recognize that giving it away to charity may be what makes some of their clients happy and fulfilled. Whatever it is, they know that they need to take the time to discover and understand. As Ross Levin, CFP®, a planner in Minneapolis and past chairman of IAFP, has written, "…true financial planning must use the necessary tactics to try to increase our chances of clients being financially successful, but it must also include evaluating all available client resources (financial, emotional, physical, spiritual) to help clients maximize their potential for happiness. I believe that this is our moral obligation as planners."

George Kinder knows that his clients are the *people* and he has a process that helps him to understand their history around money, their values, their attitudes, and their goals in life before he makes recommendations for what to do with the money. That is what good financial planners do, and it is not what the average money manager does. Financial life planning is a discipline for planners who want their clients to be people and not money.

Who are your clients? When a client calls to express concern about market volatility, what is the first thing you talk about? Is it the portfolio, or is it the client? Do you find yourself using well-worn phrases like "stay the course," "don't worry, it will bounce back" or "remember, you're in it for the long run?" Or do you ask about the client and how she is coping? Do you discuss her goals and how this fluctuation may be affecting her ability to reach them? Do you do whatever is necessary to help her to feel comfortable, even if doing so may mean a temporary retreat from equities? If you find yourself talking more about the money than the individual, you may be defining who your client really is, regardless of what you may be telling people.

QUALITATIVE AND QUANTITATIVE DISCOVERY

Several years ago, we purchased a home at the New Jersey shore that had a boat slip. We had never owned a boat before and decided that the slip looked very lonely and needed a vessel to make it (and us) happy. So we bought our first boat, a 24-foot single engine cruiser. Now, those of you who know something about boating will understand that handling a boat, particularly if it has one engine, is quite challenging (especially for a novice). I quickly learned that the only similarity to driving a car is that they both have steering wheels. Cars steer from the front, boats from the back; cars self-correct their steering, boats need to be manually steered back after turns; cars have brakes and boats don't! So learning to handle this new toy took time and practice. And the most difficult part of boat handling is maneuvering in close quarters.

In that first year, coming home and docking our boat was always an adventure and sometimes a near disaster. On this particular day, I approached the slip, carefully as usual. As I neared my destination, it became obvious that my course would result in a collision with a piling and possible damage to the boat. So I did what I was taught. I backed up, circled, and started again. My approach this time was perfect and I entered the slip better than I ever had before. Proudly, I turned to my wife, who had been silent up to now, and asked, "What do you think of that?" "It was great," she replied, "but we don't live here!"

An amusing story, perhaps, but what relevance does it have to financial planning? Well, for that first approach I had the goal correct, but my technical (quantitative) competence and skills were flawed, so the result was unsatisfactory. For my second try, my mechanics and quantitative data were perfect, but I was aiming for the wrong goal. And so it is with financial planning. Without a proper balance between the quantitative and qualitative (some label them the exterior and interior) issues, our advice may be off target.

So many of the financial service company ads we see on television and the newspapers claim that the advisers of their companies make the clients' dreams and goals "their number one priority." But check their data-gathering documents and their recommendations and you'll likely find something quite different. When an adviser's "discovery" questionnaire devotes many pages to collecting numbers and data (how much do you have, where is it invested, how much do you spend, what are the sources of your income, etc.,) and only one or two questions about goals, how can one be expected to get the boat in the right slip, except by accident?

ASKING THE RIGHT QUESTIONS

It takes a dialogue, not a questionnaire, to uncover what is really important in your clients' lives, and we will cover this in future chapters. One of my clients was being interviewed by a journalist for a story about trust and financial advice and was asked, "What questions should a person ask financial planners before hiring one?" My client answered, "It's not the questions you ask them that matter, it's the questions they ask you!" He went on to explain that "...when the first questions potential advisers ask are about your money, it should be clear that those people are, most likely, more interested in your money than they are in you. However, if the questions they ask are about you, your life, your family, and your goals, it is highly likely that will devote themselves to what is important to you." When I am interviewed by journalists who ask how to choose a financial planner, one of the things I routinely tell them is that if the first question they ask is, "How much money do you have?" politely excuse yourself and find another planner, because that person is more interested in your money than in your life.

DOING WHAT IS RIGHT FOR THE CLIENT—NOT THE PORTFOLIO

Making the fundamental decision that your client is a person and not a portfolio is the first step to merging your clients' money with their lives. Vern Hayden, who practices in New York, is a planner who gets it. One day, during the bear market of 2000–2002, I was working at home and listening to CNBC. The host announced that Vern Hayden was to be his next guest. Since I know Vern, I listened intently. The commentator introduced him by saying that Vern was going to discuss his "bunker portfolio." I know that Vern is an asset allocator, so I was surprised to hear that he was reacting to market volatility. His bunker portfolio consisted, as we would surmise, of high-quality short-term bonds. The host asked him the question I wanted to ask: "Vern, you always told me that you didn't believe in market timing. But isn't that exactly what you are doing?" Vern's answer was a perfect example of how to merge your clients' money with their lives. He replied, "I don't time the market. I time my clients!" He went on to explain that the clients he did this for had two things in common. First, their worries about the market were so pervasive that it was affecting their lives. Second, their temporary exit from equities would not have an adverse effect on their ability to reach their goals. While these clients probably missed the early months of the recovery, that was a price they were willing to pay if it meant the end of sleepless nights. And, of course, they had the knowledge (provided by their planner) that it would not affect them in the long run.

I am reminded of a client who obsessed about Y2K (remember that?) in 1999. He instructed me to sell everything that could have an adverse effect if the doom that many were predicting actually occurred. I remember discussing this with another planner who asked me if I informed him that doing so would have been dumb. "No," I told her, "I did what he asked." You see, he could have put his money in a safety deposit box and never earned another dollar and he would have still reached all of his financial goals. Was it worth staying awake at night, just because that would have been the "correct" decision for his portfolio? A money manager certainly would have recommended that. However, I am a financial life planner and need to stay focused on my mission to help my clients free themselves from money worries and reach their goals. And getting out of stocks was the correct decision for this client, if not for his money.

Therefore, the first step in developing a practice that merges your clients' money with their lives is to do an analysis of your attitudes. Are you willing and comfortable to take the time to fully understand your clients and their goals before making financial recommendations? Do you believe that knowing your clients' histories, attitudes, and values about money is important in making decisions?

Does managing relationships give you greater satisfaction than managing money? If so, then financial life planning may be for you.

In the numerous interviews I've had with planners, I have discovered a fundamental difference between advisers who practice financial life planning (regardless of what they call it) and those who don't. Those who do not practice financial life planning rely on questionnaires completed by their clients as their bases for making decisions. Those who do use dialogue to discover who their clients are and what their goals are. As Bill Bachrach, a marketing consultant to financial advisers, has said, "Values are intangible. Your job is to uncover these values-based emotions so people can see the relationship between making smart financial decisions and fulfilling their life values. It's more about life than money." In their book, *The Trusted Advisor*, Maister, Green, and Galford write: "The ability to focus on the other person is evident in virtually all of the trusted advisers we have known."

Janet Briaud, who practices in Texas, is one such adviser. She always asks new clients the question: If you could create the perfect world, what would it look like? "I can't say it is a life-changing moment when I ask, but I can say that the result is almost always positive," she says. In this case, her client was a professor at the local university, and was not considered a pleasant person by his peers. He was often depressed, sometimes angry. Janet asked her question, and after a few preliminary generalities, he suddenly began talking about life on a farm, about land that he wanted to buy, and what it would look like. He talked about how he wanted to go hunting in the countryside.

His wife was a physician in the community, and had become the most significant contributor to the couple's financial situation. But after a little exploring, Janet discovered his wife could live anywhere, and felt comfortable with her husband's goal. If he left his job, she wondered aloud, could he do consulting work to supplement the farm income? As it happened, he was an expert in the commercial aspects of raising fish. He looked around and discovered that there were many consulting opportunities all around the country.

Janet describes what happened next: "I said, 'Why not go for it?' And you could see on his face the moment he realized that this goal was not only possible and achievable, but could be done now rather than later. His whole body language and his whole way of being completely changed. He was instantly happier." Within a year and a half after they did their goal-setting, the husband and wife moved to a farm in Iowa that was exactly as he had described it.

What, Janet wondered later, had been blocking him? "I think that when you express your goals, they become closer to reality," she says. "You might have them as part of your psychological or emotional background, as part of what you want, but you don't express them. By saying it, you actually make it more real."

It is our job as financial life planners to help our clients to discover and express their dreams and goals. This is not to diminish the importance of gathering accurate quantitative data, which we know is also critical. Remember, we need to get both right to get the boat in the proper slip without causing any damage. The great ones that I know ask questions about their clients' histories, attitudes, values, transitions, and dreams. These financial life planners are passionate about discovering all they can about their clients. They use all of the information and knowledge they have discovered to make recommendations that are not only technically sound, but that also coincide with their clients' goals and values.

They merge their clients' money with their lives.

DEVELOPING A SYSTEM FOR QUALITATIVE DISCOVERY

This approach may seem more informal than simply handing a person a 30-page questionnaire and asking them to complete it for your next meeting. Nevertheless, the process requires a system and series of interview questions to ensure that you and your clients have discovered what is most important to them. You see, I believe that financial life planning and merging clients' money with their lives is so critical that it should not be left to a random tour, chance, or intuitive response alone. Just as we have a system for collecting quantitative data, we need a process that helps us to learn what is important in our clients' lives, their relationships with money, their money histories, and how money affects their life transitions. We need to have the total client experience. Therefore, the second step to help you merge your clients' money with their lives is to have a system of qualitative discovery that uncovers their unique needs.

PREPARING YOURSELF FOR FINANCIAL LIFE PLANNING

My good friend, Gayle Colman, who practices in Massachusetts, once told me, "You can only take clients as far as you are willing to take yourself." Therefore, the third step in becoming an effective financial life planner is to put yourself through the process. At a minimum, you should answer all of the questions you will find in the chapters that follow. However, you may find it more effective if you have another planner help you, since it is quite difficult to have a dialogue with yourself. For my preparation, I attended George Kinder's workshop, "The Seven Stages of Money Maturity," and Mitch Anthony's "Financial Life Planning Institute." Not only did these experiences provide me with many of the tools you will find in this book, they helped me to understand and clarify my own values, goals, and priorities regarding money. Asking your clients questions that you have answered yourself also gives you the insight, empathy, and comprehension you will need to effectively dialogue with your clients. I will often share some of my own discoveries, and that helps people feel comfortable with the process. It also creates a trust and rapport that used to take months, or even years, to develop.

If you believe that most clients articulate their most important goals when they come to your office, you may change your mind after you go through the process yourself. I know I did. I discovered that charitable giving, for example, was much more important to me than my behavior was demonstrating, and I probably would not have revealed it if I were simply asked to list my goals on a form. As a result, I have made planned-giving commitments. Since going through the process, I do not attend conferences on weekends during the summer or when a family event conflicts. You did not see me at the FPA Retreat in 2002—it was held on a summer weekend. I cancelled another important business trip in 2003 because my grandson was testing for his brown belt in karate. These changes may seem routine to many of you, but they represented a significant change in my behavior. Most importantly, I have improved the quality of my life. That is what financial life planners do for their clients. What greater mission is there?

CHAPTER 1 SUMMARY

- Remember that your client is a human being and not a portfolio.
- It takes a balance of qualitative and quantitative skills and information to "get the boat in the right slip."
- It takes a dialogue, not a questionnaire, to uncover what is important to your client.
- You need a system and series of interview questions to ensure that you and your clients have discovered what is most important to them.
- You can only take clients as far as you are willing to take yourself.

2

Why Good Advisers Often Give Bad Advice: The Danger of Assumptions

*Preconceived notions are the locks
on the door to wisdom.*

—Merry Browne

Two cars were being driven fast and in opposite directions along a winding country road. The brush alongside the road was so high that it made it almost impossible to see around corners. One of the cars was being driven by a man and the other by a woman. As they approached a bend at high speeds, they only just managed to see each other in time and averted a tragedy. As they passed each other, the woman shouted to the man, "Pig!" He yelled back, "Cow!" He accelerated around the corner and hit a pig. This is a good example of how erroneous assumptions can get us in trouble!

It is certainly no different for many financial advisers. It's like the story about the fisherman whose small boat comes up to the dock and he unloads a few fish. A financial adviser asks, "How long did it take you to catch those fish?" "Only a little while," the fisherman replies. "Why didn't you stay out longer so you could catch more fish?" the adviser asks. "What I have here is enough." "What do you do with the rest of your time?" "I sleep late, spend time with my family, visit friends, and read." The financial adviser tells the fisherman he could spend more time fishing, buy a bigger boat, set up a fishing empire, and become wealthy. "How long would that take?" asks the fisherman. "Oh, about 10 or 15 years." "Then what?" "Here's the best part," says the adviser. "You can just do a little fishing each day and spend the rest of your time with family and friends doing the things you enjoy." "Really," replied the fisherman, "that is exactly what I have now. Why would I want to wait 10 or 15 years to enjoy my life?" The financial adviser did not have an answer.

GOOD ADVISERS—BAD ADVICE

How many times have you observed other professionals offering the wrong advice to their clients because of assumptions they made about the clients' needs or wants? Not too long ago, I accompanied my clients, a married couple, to their attorney's office for a revision of their estate plan. While it was the first time I met the attorney, the clients had used his services before and were satisfied with his work. Moreover, the attorney's credentials indicated that he was extremely knowledgeable. This was not a complex situation, and required the normal unified credit trust, powers of attorney, health care powers, etc. What concerned me was that the attorney—without asking any questions about how my clients felt about anything—proceeded to tell them what they needed. He said he was going to draft a Q-TIP Trust ("You want to have ultimate control over who eventually gets your assets"). "Family members," he told them, "make poor trustees, so we will have to name a corporate trustee." He even declared how they should provide income for their children. "The last thing you want to do is provide any income to your children until they are 25." Rather than simple durable powers of attorney, the ones he was going to draft would have required the signatures of two doctors before they became effective. "You certainly don't want your spouse to have unfettered access to your money," he said, as if he knew the answer to the question he never asked. He justified all of these "recommendations"—which were more like directives—by informing them that his personal estate plan had the same provisions! This practitioner was following what we might call the "Fool's Golden Rule"—do unto others assuming they are just like you.

My clients left that day with the attorney's estate plan—except their names would have been on the documents. Several days later, I met with them to discuss their estate plan, and asked the questions their attorney should have asked. "How do you feel about leaving money to your children? If something were to happen to both of you, at what age would you want your children to begin receiving income? How about principal? Do either of you want ultimate control over who will eventually get your assets, or would you prefer to leave that decision to the surviving spouse? Do you feel comfortable with the requirement that two doctors must sign a statement affirming your disability before you can exercise your power of attorney? Would you want to give the surviving spouse the ability to withdraw 5 percent of the principal each year? Is there a family member with whom you would be comfortable serving as trustee or co-trustee? Do either of you want to make charitable bequests?"

Their answers to these questions convinced them to call their attorney to instruct him to revise the plan to reflect their desires. They changed the distribution schedules for their children, requested powers of attorney that did not require any doctors' signatures, and made a bequest to their church. When I asked them why they did not speak up at the meeting, they told me that their attorney was the expert and they were just going along with his recommendations. His technical expertise was fine, but he lost sight of the goal of estate planning, which is implementing the *clients'* desires—not his. He got the boat in the wrong slip! When we dispense advice, we must always remember that our clients rely on us to do what is best for them. Many of them may implement recommendations that may not represent their desires simply because they believe that we "know best." This attorney made assumptions about his clients that clouded his ability to give good advice.

Assumptions—even if true 90 percent of the time—are dangerous because they allow us to believe we can do the thinking and feeling for our clients.

Often, these assumptions are the culprits that hinder us from connecting with clients and prospective clients. Moreover, they often result in competent advisers giving bad advice. Most of the time you do not need to check that you are in the right boat slip, but wouldn't you feel foolish if you missed the slip 10 percent of the time?

THE DANGER OF ASSUMPTIONS

Rick Kahler, a financial life planner who practices in South Dakota, tells a story about an estate planning proposal he made about ten years ago. The assumption he made was that everyone's primary goal when planning their estate was to save taxes, so his recommendations were driven by that assumption. They never implemented the plan and, in fact, did not return as clients. However, he developed a personal relationship with the husband and recently invited the couple to lunch. Rick describes what happened. "I was explaining how I used to be so focused on the numbers (I had totally forgotten about their case or my presentation), had changed my ways and how important the interior (qualitative) issues were. The wife responded, 'Rick, don't you remember? That is why we never returned to you ten years ago to complete our planning. You were so focused on saving us taxes on our estate that you never bothered to ask what was important to us.'" Right execution—wrong boat slip! How many of us continue to approach planning the way Rick did ten years ago? After all, isn't that what we were trained to do? How much of our formal education was devoted to meaningful discovery? If we are to provide client-centered advice that is based on our clients' unique goals, we need to discard those assumptions that seem to influence so many of our recommendations.

Bob Barry, a former president of FPA, observes,

Under the old model of a pre-life planning approach, we focused much more on what money could do for people than on what they wanted from their lives and how the totality of their resources, not just their money, could provide them the best possible setting. We also continued to be surprised when there was a 'change of course' that clients precipitously took in their lives. It became clear that a change in how we held our conversations with clients would have led us to make different conclusions about where clients were in their lives and where they were headed.

TYPICAL ASSUMPTIONS MADE BY ADVISERS

Every aspect of financial planning has the potential for built-in assumptive baggage. We have all met estate planning attorneys who approach every relationship as if saving estate taxes is a god whom everyone should worship. Sadly, not very many ask thought-provoking questions such as, "How do you want to be remembered?" Or accountants who recommend that clients increase their mortgage debt or even purchase a second home to save income taxes. How about asking them, "How do you feel about debt?" I attended an estate planning session at one of the national conferences and the speaker, a prominent attorney, proclaimed, "I never recommend 'five and five' powers in trusts, because I don't believe in them." Is what his clients believe of any importance to him? He certainly would have gotten it wrong in my situation because, with full knowledge of the advantages and disadvantages of providing these powers, I opted to include the provision in my trust. The estate planner's job, perhaps his fiduciary duty, is to inform his clients of the facts, and do what they want—regardless of his personal beliefs. This lawyer makes the erroneous assumption that everyone feels the same way he does.

Financial planners may also find themselves making assumptions because they do not probe deeply enough to discover their clients' real life goals and values. How many questionnaires ask, "When do you plan to retire?" What does that assume? Or, "What will your children's college expenses be?" without asking the follow-up question, "How much, if any, do you plan to pay?" There are planners who recommend survivorship insurance in all cases where estate taxes will be due at death. How often do we recommend a profit-sharing plan that provides the lion's share of the benefit (such as 80 percent) to the business owner without asking her how she feels about providing benefits for her employees? And how many of our clients' portfolios look exactly like ours? Our profession brings along with it a terrific weight of responsibility. Just as my clients did not share their feelings and were willing to defer their own intentions and feelings to the "expertise" of the attorney, so many other clients act in tacit agreement with our ideas—whether they fit or not. This process is not about our ideas as much as it is about the lives of our clients. Our job, as planners, is to tailor our strategies to better support their lives.

Assumptions, no matter how many times you have seen them affirmed, are thin ice for serving clients and building relationships.

GETTING IT RIGHT FOR THE CLIENT

When I met Janice, she had recently been widowed, and was virtually frozen in her life. She was only in her forties, had no children, and had relied on her husband for handling their finances. She also worked in his professional practice. When he died, she lost a friend, lover, employer, and financial adviser. Feeling hopeless, she was seeing a therapist, but progress was slow. When I tried to probe to discover her goals, her response was, "I have none." However, the discovery process revealed that she did want to simplify her life. She had inherited several commercial real estate properties and wanted to relieve herself of the burdens of management. Therefore, we developed a plan for selling the properties and took over her investment portfolio. Several months later, she called and there was enthusiasm and excitement in her voice for the first time. A small retail specialty shop in her neighborhood was available for sale and she asked me about the feasibility of buying it. She was quite familiar with the area and the store and knew the owner very well. When we discussed her motivation, she told me that it would give her a purpose in life—something that was missing since her husband's death. The price was not very high and she had more than enough money to afford it. She asked for my recommendation and I told her to go for it.

Shortly after my conversation, I got a call from the business broker who said that her banker told Janice that it was not a very good deal. He told her that real estate would be a better investment. Financially, that may or not have been a wise decision, but that banker *assumed* that she was considering this transaction solely for financial gain. I knew differently, but he never bothered to ask. She was about to enter a new phase of her life, from a mourning widow who felt as if she had no reason to live to an excited business owner with a purpose to her life. Moreover, as we had previously agreed, my client was in the process of *selling* her commercial real estate to simplify her life. She certainly was not contemplating buying another property. He may have been giving her what he believed was good financial advice, but he missed the boat slip! I based my recommendation on the knowledge that it was going to change my client's life—not her net worth! Once again, we have an example of an adviser making erroneous assumptions that result in bad advice.

Several months later, an estate planning attorney, who was revising Janice's documents, called me. He asked me how I felt about family limited partnerships. More specifically, how did I feel about one for Janice? I asked him why he would recommend this tactic to someone who had no children and whose primary beneficiary was her 82-year-old mother. His assumptive answer was, "to save taxes." I reminded him that simplifying her life was one of her primary goals and a FLP would not accomplish that objective. Actually, this strategy would have complicated her life! His intention seemed to be to demonstrate that he had the technical knowledge to recommend sophisticated solutions.

These advisers based their advice on the assumptions they made, rather than the information they could have had if they had taken the time to ask.

Mitch Anthony tells of a call he received from a planner who told him that Mitch needed to start thinking about preparing for retirement. Mitch's response was, "Let me ask you a question. This morning, I got up and read for awhile— I love to read—wrote for an hour or two—I love to write— then got on the phone with clients that I genuinely like, played nine holes at lunch hour, and then made a few more calls. All this was sandwiched between taking my kids to and from school. My question is, 'What exactly do you want me to retire from?'" This planner assumed either that Mitch did not like his work and wanted to quit or that he had bigger, more important plans that he was not pursuing. He did not know how to deal with the fact that he was talking to someone who was already living his passion and had no plans for quitting. Rather than asking Mitch about his life goals, he assumed that everyone (including Mitch) wants to retire. *Wrong boat slip again!*

A client called to ask for my opinion on whether he should implement a recommendation he received from his banker to refinance his 7 percent, $72,000 mortgage (with 6 years remaining) with a 6 percent, $220,000, 15-year mortgage. His advice was to use the extra money to pay for my client's educational expenses for his children. The banker never bothered to discover that this client had already set aside money in a 529 plan to pay his children's tuition. Moreover, he was looking forward to being debt-free. This was another example of lack of meaningful discovery! More erroneous assumptions—more bad advice.

NOT ALL FINANCIAL DECISIONS ARE FINANCIAL

I once read an article in one of the industry publications about the feasibility of taking money from a portfolio to pay off a mortgage. The author described, in painful detail, the variables that should be considered. He discussed various portfolio allocations, standard deviations, and listed probabilities of success for each. It was a highly competent piece, but nowhere in that article did the author suggest asking your client the most important, if not the only, question to help to make the decision: *"How do you feel about debt?"* As financial life planners, we need to understand that not all decisions involving money are financial. When clients ask me if it would be prudent to pay off their mortgage, I ask them to ponder what would make them feel more comfortable or secure—being free of debt with less money in the portfolio or maintaining the debt and the additional money. In many of these cases, the client is merely looking for your approval to do something they would like to do and which their accountant may have told them was "stupid."

At a workshop I recently facilitated for T.D. Waterhouse clients, I was discussing how qualitative discovery is at the core of all good advice, and that assumptions by advisers may result in bad advice. One of the participants shared that she was very uncomfortable with her mortgage debt, wanted to pay it off, and had the resources to do so. However, her accountant advised her that she should not do that because she needed the tax deduction. In other words, he convinced her that her satisfaction and peace of mind were not nearly as important as that tax write-off. Each year when they met, she would disclose her discomfort, and each year the advice never changed. "Keep the debt," she was told, "or lose the valuable deduction." While this decision did not feel right to her, she followed his advice because, as she said, "That's why I hired him." I could not have created a clearer example of quantitative advice gone astray than the one shared by this woman. Her accountant assumed that saving income taxes was her goal, because it was his. By the way, the last piece of information she disclosed was her age. She was 81 years old! While I have never met this adviser, to paraphrase Oscar Wilde, some people know the cost of everything but the value of nothing.

ASKING THE QUESTIONS OTHERS DON'T

Several years ago, I had a meeting in my conference room with a client (John), his accountant, and his business attorney to evaluate a proposal to purchase his business submitted by one of his employees. John owned a company that bought used parts, reconditioned them, and sold them. It was quite successful, but he said he wanted to retire and felt that one of his key employees, Dave, could take over. The offering price was considerably below market and the conversation, being led by his other advisers, centered on price and a counteroffer.

I sensed that John was feeling uneasy about the process. I knew that he liked to discuss deals he recently made, so I asked if he had recently consummated any. He became very animated and described a purchase he had just put together. It was clear that he was excited and thoroughly enjoyed the process. So I asked the question that no one had bothered to ask, "John, why do you want to retire?" He thought for a while and answered that he no longer enjoyed many of the things he had to do, such as hiring, training, supervising, staying current on administration, technology, etc. "But," he said, "I love to do the deals!" So I asked, "John, have you ever considered keeping the business, giving Dave a significant raise, and asking him to be accountable for all of those responsibilities that you hate doing while you continue to do what you love—the deals?" His entire countenance changed, because the conversation was now shifting to what he wanted to do, not the valuation of his business. After a brief discussion about how he could implement the strategy, he said that was exactly what he wanted to do. His other advisers acted as if they were not in the room while this dialogue was taking place, and they resumed the previous conversation about counteroffers. Frustrated, he stopped them, banged on the conference table, and shouted, "No, I want to do what Roy said."

In many cases, as we will demonstrate throughout this book, many of our clients, like John, do not understand what they really want. And no planner, no matter how conscientious, can help clients reach their goals until the client discovers what those true goals are. It is our job to help them to discover them by asking questions and *assuming nothing.*

John's other advisers may have been doing what they

were trained to do, but any training process that ignores good discovery is flawed. It is the foundation upon which great financial planning is built! Yet, these advisers continued to give advice based on their flawed assumptions—even after John communicated what he really wanted very clearly. It has been five years since that meeting in our conference room, and John is still doing the deals!

ASSUME NOTHING

No matter how smart we are, how well trained we are, or how experienced we are, it does not give us the right to think for others or, more importantly, to assume how others might feel. We should assume nothing. We must explore beyond the superficial and let our clients tell us what they want, what they need, and how they want it to happen. Even if we feel absolutely sure about what they need and why they need it, we must ask anyway. If they are ambiguous, and they ask for our opinions, we can offer them an epilogue stating, "Just because it feels right for me doesn't necessarily mean it will feel right for you."

Assumptions get in the way of good financial planning because they prevent us from asking the questions that reveal what a client's true goals are. If our advice is to be client-centered, it needs to reflect the client's wishes and not the adviser's assumptions!

CHAPTER 2 SUMMARY
- Beware of the Fool's Golden Rule… do unto others assuming they are just like you.
- Assumptions are dangerous. They prevent us from connecting with clients.
- Assumptions often result in good advisers giving bad advice.

- Assumptions prevent us from asking the questions that reveal what the client's true goals are.
- To be client-centered is to reflect the client's wishes, not the adviser's assumptions.

3 | *The Initial Interview—Helping Clients Find a Home*

It is better to know some of the questions than all of the answers.

—James Thurber

Before building our new home several years ago, my wife, Peggy, and I interviewed two architects who were recommended to us by our builder. In the initial interview with the first architect, he asked about the square footage, size of the rooms, number of rooms and baths, roofline, garage size, etc. Of course, these were very important issues and we needed to deal with them at some point. However, it was obvious to us when we discussed the architect's approach that his emphasis was primarily on the technical aspects of building a house. The interview with the second architect was quite different. She asked about our lifestyle, how often we entertained, whether we preferred formal or informal surroundings, what we intended to do outdoors, etc. From the questions these architects asked in their initial interviews, we concluded that the first architect was interested in building a *house*, and the second wanted to help us create a *home*. Of course, we hired the second architect, and our home is exactly as we dreamed it would be.

FIRST IMPRESSIONS—SETTING THE STAGE

As with the first architect with whom we met, we all know the importance of first impressions. But how many of us have taken the time to reflect on what we communicate about our role during that key first meeting? The context you establish in your initial interview with prospective clients sets the stage for the kind of experience they will expect from you. If your initial questions are about taxes, investments, estate planning, and other quantitative issues and you take little or no time to get to know who your prospective clients are, you may be giving the impression that you are more interested in constructing a house than in building a home. You may represent yourself as a planner who genuinely cares about your clients, but your initial questions will enlighten them about whether you care more about their money than their lives. The first questions you ask need to be about their families, goals, expectations, and dreams. There will be ample time at later sessions to gather quantitative information. The purpose of this first meeting is to get to know your prospective client, to communicate that your process is centered on accomplishing their unique needs, and to begin to develop rapport.

THE JIGSAW PUZZLE

Elizabeth Jetton, CFP®, former president of FPA, who practices in Atlanta, communicates her planning process by asking prospective clients if they have ever built a jigsaw puzzle.

When they say they have, she follows up by asking, "What is
the most important piece of the puzzle?" Most people
respond, "The corners." "Not really," Elizabeth replies, "the
most important piece is the picture on the box!" By opening
the dialogue in this manner, Elizabeth is expressing to her
clients that the technical aspects of planning, while important, will be of little benefit unless she understands the end
goals. She hasn't made the quantitative phase of planning less
important (how would one complete a jigsaw puzzle by simply staring at the picture on the box?), but she has set the
stage for a holistic, client-centered planning experience.

Emerson wrote, "What you do speaks so loud that I
cannot hear what you say." You cannot fake sincerity. The
first architect we met with claimed that he was dedicated
to building our dream home. However, his questions and
attitude belied that statement, and we left believing that we
were in for a technical experience about square footage,
building materials, number of rooms, etc. We felt unsure
that he would give any thought to our needs and desires.
This may have been a harsh judgment, but we were not
willing to take the chance. You need to be careful what you
discuss during the initial consultation because this important first encounter will set the stage for what your clients
may expect if they hire you. If you claim that you are a
planner who is dedicated to understanding their goals and
dreams and helping them fulfill them, you do not communicate that by asking for quantitative data before you ask
about who they are and what their goals are. Since "you
don't get a second chance to make a first impression,"
financial life planners need to make it clear in this first
meeting that they do not make recommendations in a technical vacuum. The first step in planning is to know what

our clients want their futures to look like. We need to see the picture on the jigsaw puzzle box. More important, our clients need to see, *perhaps for the first time in their lives*, the picture of the future they want to build for themselves.

YOUR FIRST COMMUNICATION

The communication process begins when a prospective client calls to schedule an initial consultation. Most people will ask what they should take with them to the meeting. This is your first, and perhaps your only, opportunity to set yourself apart from the pure technicians. If you ask them to bring investment statements, wills, budgets, and tax returns, you may be sending the message that what they own is more important to you than who they are. We send them a "Financial Life Checkup" (see Exhibit 1), developed by Mitch Anthony and adapted by our firm. It asks 20 questions about their feelings regarding specific financial aspects of their lives. We ask them to bring the completed survey—and themselves—because that is all we will need for this first get-acquainted meeting. The process of demonstrating how you approach planning begins with your answer to this simple request. You need to let them know that getting to understand them is the first important step in establishing a planning relationship.

We send one questionnaire for each spouse/partner to complete. This sends two important messages to our prospective clients: that we are interested in knowing how they feel about money and that our process will engage both spouses. It may seem obvious, but I have met far too many financial planners who act as if couples have unified feelings and opinions about money. Their discovery documents are designed for couples—not individuals—to answer the questions. Even if they have similar feelings, each spouse will want to feel cared about and desire a rapport with the planner. I actually had a wife tell me that I was the first financial adviser she met who actually cared about and listened to what she had to say.

Of course, we know that spouses may feel quite differently about their finances. During a recent initial consultation, the husband answered that he felt very satisfied with their ability to meet their financial obligations (he scored it a "5"), but his wife was very concerned (her score for the same question was "2"). How does one reconcile the disparity? After all, they share the same financial situation. Is it possible to discover these feelings by examining a tax return or an investment statement? Or what if we asked the couple the question? It is very likely that the dominant personality would answer the question and the other's feelings would not be discovered. Since we believe it is important to understand differences as well as similarities in feelings before dispensing advice, we ask each spouse these and all other qualitative questions.

OPENING THE DIALOGUE

Before discussing the completed Financial Life Checkup questionnaires, we begin the meeting by asking each spouse to "tell me about yourself." This open-ended question can be quite revealing because it often provides us with clues about what is important in their lives. Some people launch into a discussion about their careers, while others may talk about their families. Whatever they communicate, it is a great icebreaker. As we know, people love to talk about themselves. In addition, it lets our potential clients know that we are interested in them and it helps us to understand what they value most. Our next questions are:

- Why are you here?
- What are your goals?
- What do you expect from a relationship with a financial planner?

The purpose of these questions is to begin to establish a dialogue and build rapport. While the goal (and result) of this meeting may be a new client relationship, it is very important that your potential clients do not feel as if they are in a sales meeting. This discussion needs to be about them more than you and your company. Demonstrating how clever you are and how much technical expertise you have may be a very good tactic for beginning a monologue, but it is no way to begin a dialogue. D.J. Kaufman wrote, "Wisdom is the reward for a lifetime of listening... when you'd have preferred to talk."

THE FINANCIAL LIFE CHECKUP

Our next step is to discuss the Financial Life Checkup. We have found that it is always better to begin by asking them to tell us about the areas where they feel positive about money and what they have done to make that happen. People are more likely to open up about their positive experiences than their negative ones. After a brief conversation about these topics, we ask about their concerns. We probe further to discover what, if any, actions they have taken to resolve them, and why they believe their strategies have not resolved the problems. It is extremely important not to be judgmental at this time, because clients need to feel safe if we expect them to share their issues and deepest concerns.

This discovery process also opens up a rich dialogue, and begins to form a foundation for the relationship going forward. People begin to understand that this engagement will be about who they are—not just what they have.

ABOUT YOUR FIRM

Only after listening to clients share their stories and feeding back your understanding of what they have told you, should you discuss how your firm works with clients, what they might expect, and how you may be able to help them. But they first need to be reminded that money is a means to an end, and growing it for the sake of accumulating wealth (that they may never need) is what causes many people to lose sleep over market fluctuations. If someone seems concerned about "beating the market," I may ask, "Have you ever given any thought to what relevance that has to reaching your goals?" "If the S&P is not a member of your family," I jokingly ask, "why would you be concerned about what it does every day? What if we determine that you need 8 percent to reach your goals and the S&P returns 5 percent over 20 years? Will you be happy if you earn 6 percent, even if this means you did not achieve your goals? On the other hand, if you could reach every financial goal you have in your life by buying six-month CDs, would you expose your money to any risk?" While these may be extreme examples, they clearly demonstrate to these prospective clients that the objective of financial life planning is to help them reach their goals, this helps them to distinguish the difference between a money manager and a financial life planner. Both have value, but one is computing success by investment performance while the other measures success by how well the client's needs are being met. Managing their assets may be one of the strategies to accomplish their objectives, but it is not the goal in and of itself. Money, we remind them, makes a wonderful servant but a poor master.

If we do not get agreement on these basic principles, and prospective clients insist that getting above-market returns is what is most important in their lives, we politely tell them that they are probably in the wrong office and that they should seek the advice of a money manager. I am often asked by other advisers what we do if a potential client does not want to go through the process and just wants us to invest and manage the money. I asked this question of every planner I interviewed for this book, and their responses (as is mine) were that they simply do not take the client. As Shakespeare wrote, "This above all: to thine own self be true, and it must follow, as the night the day, thou canst not then be false to any man."

PREPARATION FOR THE NEXT MEETING

If they are comfortable with our approach, our next step is to describe the entire process, from the first client meeting to continuing service. We quote our fee, and if they agree to go ahead, we give each of them the following question-naires to complete:

- Dreams, Visions, and Images for Use of Wealth, developed by George Kinder, CFP®, and adapted by Cecily Maton, CFP®, a financial planner in Chicago, and Ed Jacobson, Ph.D., a psychologist. (see Exhibit 2)
- Defining True Wealth (see Exhibit 3)
- Life Transitions Profile (adapted by our firm from material developed by Mitch Anthony) (see Exhibit 4)
- Benevolence Survey (see Exhibit 5)

No quantitative data is requested at this time. We tell our new clients the first meetings will be devoted to learning about their histories, values, attitudes, and goals about money. It is important to follow up on what they were told to expect, and we believe it would send the wrong signal to begin the process by collecting numbers, schedules, and documents. The initial client meeting defines the experience and expectation for clients going forward and describes the degree of value you can add to your clients' lives. A rich opening dialogue enables you to define yourself and build rapport. It also allows your prospective clients to begin to express themselves and what is important to them.

You need to decide if you are in the business of assembling houses or building dream homes, and ensure that your initial dialogue sets the stage for the relationship you want and the experience your clients desire. When prospects come to see you with their sticks and bricks, it may be tempting to jump right in and begin to describe what you could build with the materials they bring. However, we do not believe that clients are coming to you to have a house built—they are looking for a place to call home with their financial life.

NEXT STEPS

In addition to scheduling the next meeting, we need to summarize the process. At our firm, the process, which will be described in detail in future chapters, is as follows:

I. First Client Meeting
   A. Review and discuss the above questionnaires
   B. Discover clients' histories and values about money
   C. Discover clients' dreams and preliminary goals

      D. Give them quantitative data-gathering form and risk tolerance questionnaire to complete next meeting

II. Second Client Meeting

      A. Prioritize goals

      B. Determine the resources necessary to accomplish the clients' goals

      C. Discover tolerance for volatility

      D. Investment education

III. Third Client Meeting

      A. Review quantitative data

      B. Project the financial feasibility of reaching each goal

      C. Discuss issues in estate planning, taxes, cash flow, funding for education and other large expenditures, risk management, etc.

IV. Fourth Client Meeting

      A. Make specific recommendations (cash flow, income taxes, risk management, legacy, investments, estate planning, etc.)

      B. Help to implement recommendations

      C. Agree on next steps

CHAPTER 3 SUMMARY

- The questions you ask in your initial meetings with prospective clients will set the stage for the client-planner relationship.
- The most important piece of a jigsaw puzzle is the picture on the box.
- Avoid asking prospective clients to bring quantitative data to the initial consultation.
- Have each spouse/partner complete a Financial Life Checkup as preparation for your first meeting.
- Begin the dialogue by asking open-ended questions, such

as, "Tell me about yourself."
- Remind people that money is a means to an end.
- Accept only those clients who are comfortable with your planning process.
- To prepare for the next meeting, have clients complete qualitative questionnaires.
- Financial life planners build dream homes.

EXHIBIT 1:

Financial Life Checkup

Name _____ Date _____

Directions: The statements below will help you to think about and assess how satisfied you are with the aspects of your life.

Not Satisfied	Moderately Satisfied	Very Satisfied
1	2 3	4 5

	I am satisfied...	
1	...with my ability to meet my financial obligations.	⬭
2	...with the income potential my current job or career provides me.	⬭
3	...with my spending habits.	⬭
4	...with the level of debt I carry.	⬭
5	...with the "extras" that I am able to buy for myself and/or loved ones.	⬭
6	...with the level and quality of insurance protection I currently have.	⬭
7	...with the amount of money that I save and invest on a regular basis.	⬭
8	...with my current investment choices.	⬭
9	...that I am on track to build a sufficient retirement nest egg.	⬭
10	...with the level of employee benefits I receive.	⬭
11	...with my style of personal bookkeeping and financial records management.	⬭
12	...with my plans for my children's education.	⬭
13	...with my estate plan.	⬭
14	...with my level of charitable giving.	⬭
15	...with the level of personal financial education I have attained.	⬭
16	...with how I respond emotionally to my personal finance issues.	⬭
17	...with my ability to communicate about my financial matters.	⬭
18	...with the feelings I have about my money life.	⬭
19	...that financial issues do not cause stress or strain in the relationships that are important to me.	⬭
20	...with the working relationships I have with my financial service providers (that is, insurance agent, banker, financial planner, broker, and accountant).	⬭
	Total	

Financial Life Planning ™

EXHIBIT 2:

Dreams, Visions, Images
For Use of Wealth

Name:_____ Date:_____

In the table below, you will find a number of possible uses to which you could put
your current or future wealth. For each one, please place an "X" in *one* of the three
boxes to the right based upon the following definitions:

> **Heart's Core:** *a deeply held core value of yours,* as to how the
> wealth should be used. This is a value that you "stand for."

> **Ought To:** something *you feel obligated to do,* based on a commit-
> ment you may have made or a belief held by your family, someone
> outside your family, or society in general.

> **Fun To:** the "icing on the cake." Doing this would add zest or spice
> to your life, *is not an obligation you feel,* and is not truly a deeply
> held core value, but it sure would be fun!

POSSIBLE USES OF YOUR WEALTH	Heart's Core	Ought To	Fun To	N/A
Providing for my family's ongoing needs (Note: this involves day-to-day living expense, mortgage and car payments, vacations, funding children's education, etc.)				
Supporting parents, sibs, other family members in need				
Providing an inheritance for my children				
Adjusting selected elements of current lifestyle (a second home, a boat, an airplane, traveling, an "expensive hobby," etc.)				
Supporting a major change in my work and career				
Actualizing a very different direction for my life				
Charitable giving/philanthropy				
Other(s)—please specify				

EXHIBIT 3:

Defining True Wealth

Name:_____   Date:_____

1. I define success in my working life as:

_____
_____
_____
_____

2. I define success in my family life as:

_____
_____
_____
_____

3. I define balance in my life as:

_____
_____
_____
_____

4. I define success in my financial life as:

_____
_____
_____
_____

5. I hope to be remembered someday as:

_____
_____
_____
_____

EXHIBIT 4:

Life Transitions Profile
Family

Name:_____   Date:_____

Mark an **X** (under "select") in any transition that is applicable to your life.
For each selected transition, please fill in the appropriate time frame and priority code.

Time Frame: C = Current   **N** = Near Term (1–5 years)   **L** = Long Term (Over 5 years)
Priority Code: 1 = Lowest   **2** = Medium-low   **3** = Medium   **4** = Medium-high   **5** = Highest

Life Transitions	Select (X)	Time Frame C	N	L	Priority Code 1	2	3	4	5
Change in marital status									
Expecting or adopting a child									
Child with special needs (disability/other)									
Helping and/or gifting to children/grandchildren									
Concern about health or family member									
Family member needs care giving									
Concern about personal health									
Provide for personal long-term care									
Other_____									
Other_____									
Other_____									
Other_____									

EXHIBIT 4 *(CONTINUED)*:

Life Transitions Profile
Work/Career

Name:_____   Date:_____

Mark an **X** (under "select") in any transition that is applicable to your life.
For each selected transition, please fill in the appropriate time frame and priority code.

Time Frame: **C** = Current   **N** = Near Term (1–5 years)   **L** = Long Term (Over 5 years)
Priority Code: 1 = Lowest   **2** = Medium-low   **3** = Medium   **4** = Medium-high   **5** = Highest

Life Transitions	Select (X)	Time Frame C	N	L	Priority Code 1	2	3	4	5
Change in career path									
Job loss									
Job restructure									
Education/retraining									
Sell or close business									
Transfer family business									
Gain/lose a business partner									
Downshift/simplify work life									
Sabbatical/leave of absence									
Start or purchase a business									
Retire									
Other_____									
Other_____									
Other_____									
Other_____									

EXHIBIT 4 *(CONTINUED):*

Life Transitions Profile
Financial

Name:_____   Date:_____

Mark an **X** (under "select") in any transition that is applicable to your life.
For each selected transition, please fill in the appropriate time frame and priority code.

Time Frame: C = Current   **N** = Near Term (1–5 years)   **L** = Long Term (Over 5 years)
Priority Code: 1 = Lowest **2** = Medium-low **3** = Medium **4** = Medium-high **5** = Highest

Life Transitions	Select (X)	Time Frame			Priority Code				
		C	N	L	1	2	3	4	5
Purchase/sell a home									
Relocate to another area									
Purchase a vacation home/time share									
Consider investment opportunity									
Receive inheritance or financial windfall									
Sell assets (other than residence)									
Other_____									
Other_____									
Other_____									
Other_____									

EXHIBIT 4 *(CONTINUED)*:

Life Transitions Profile
Charitable/Legacy

Name:_____   Date:_____

Mark an **X** (under "select") in any transition that is applicable to your life.
For each selected transition, please fill in the appropriate time frame and priority code.

Time Frame: C = Current   **N** = Near Term (1–5 years)   **L** = Long Term (Over 5 years)
Priority Code: 1 = Lowest **2** = Medium-low **3** = Medium **4** = Medium-high **5** = Highest

Life Transitions	Select (X)	Time Frame			Priority Code				
		C	N	L	1	2	3	4	5
Increase charitable giving									
Develop/change estate plan									
Create and/or fund a foundation									
Create and/or fund a scholarship fund									
Consider other tax forward methods of giving									
Other_____									
Other_____									
Other_____									
Other_____									

EXHIBIT 5:

Benevolence Survey
An act of kindness, a generous gift

Name:_____   Date:_____

1. Charities or causes into which I feel a need to invest my time and energy:

_____

_____

_____

_____

2. Charities or causes to which I currently contribute:

_____

_____

_____

_____

3. Causes that I would like to support on a perpetual or annual basis:

_____

_____

_____

_____

4. Charities that I would like to provide for in my will:

_____

_____

_____

_____

5. Endowment funds I would like to establish:

_____

_____

_____

_____

4 Understanding Your Clients' Histories, Values, and Transitions

The voyage of discovery is not in seeking new landscapes but in having new eyes.

—Marcel Proust, French novelist

Ross Levin, CFP®, wrote in the *Journal of Financial Planning,* "There are a number of people out there calling themselves financial planners who are probably not really doing financial planning. They may be doing pieces of the plan, but they are not trying to discover what the client's true motivations are. They may excel at some of the tactics, but they may lack the willingness to dive deep into the client's personality to try to make sure that the plan is unique to the needs of the person for whom it is being developed… These practitioners serve a useful purpose and provide a service, but… they can mess up a client. They can get in the way of what a financial planning relationship can be like."[1]

DREAMS, VISIONS, IMAGES FOR USES OF WEALTH

Since your clients' values about money affect many of the decisions they make, one of our missions as financial life planners is to uncover and understand those values. We begin this first client discovery meeting by discussing their answers to the Dreams, Visions, and Images for Use of Wealth worksheet we introduced in the last chapter. This helps us to identify some of their core values about how they use their money. People's goals are a reflection of their personal values, and values change very little over time. They are a manifestation of clients' personal beliefs and affect the way they use their money. This exercise also facilitates the discovery of any disconnects there might be between their actions and what they say is important. For example, they may list providing an inheritance for their children as something they ought to do and philanthropy as a heart's core belief. Yet, when we ask them about their estate plans, we learn that they are leaving their entire estate to their children and no money to charity. They may be doing what they feel obligated to do rather than following their core values. We also want to know what they would like to do just for fun. Financial planning is a serious matter, but doing it properly should also make room for goals that would just be fun to accomplish. The questions we will ask later in this meeting will be in greater depth, but discussing their answers to this questionnaire is a good way to start the dialogue. In addition, the insights we gain from this simple exercise will help when we clarify their goals.

VISION OF THE FUTURE

When we are discovering our clients' goals, we need to remember, as we pointed out in the previous chapter, to avoid assumptions. For example, the question, "When do you plan to retire?" assumes a goal that the client may not have. Yet, that question is present in virtually all of the client questionnaires I have reviewed. We need to be open to listening to our clients and learning what they want their futures to look like—with or without retirement. By presuming that retirement is part of that future, we may be placing constraints on their willingness to open up about what they really want. Therefore, our first question is, "How do you visualize your life in your sixties, seventies, eighties, and later?" We want to know if they plan on retiring or anticipate any other major changes in their lifestyles. What are their greatest fears about the future? What do they most look forward to? What do they want to accomplish and experience in their lifetimes? Discussing these issues helps them to understand that retirement is a life event—not a financial destination. For many of our clients, it is the first time they have really considered what their lives might look like in the future.

LIFE TRANSITIONS PROFILE

Since proper planning also needs to include strategies for current and future transitions, we begin that dialogue by using the exercise (the Life Transitions Profile from the last chapter) they completed as a guide. As we know, most people who seek the advice of financial planners do so when they are experiencing some life transition. It may be the birth of a child, a change in marital status, an investment opportunity, or the offer of a "golden handshake." If the event is imminent, we may be forced to make or change plans without the benefit of planning's friend— *time!* We have discovered two major benefits of using a tool such as this. It helps us and our clients prepare financially for these transitions and reduce unpleasant surprises. More important than that, however, may be the fact that it teaches our clients to be thinking about the future in areas that are not as obvious as retiring at a certain date or educating children. John Lennon wrote in one of his songs, "Before you cross the street, take my hand. Life is what happens to you while you're busy making other plans." We need to prepare, as much as we can, for the events that occur in our clients' lives.

At an annual meeting with one of my clients, a 72-year-old widow, I discovered a future transition that concerned her. She lived alone in an apartment and, even though she had an excellent long-term care insurance policy, she was considering moving into a total-care facility "sometime in the future." Further probing revealed that her two sons were also very concerned. She had been gifting large sums to help her daughter, and they were worried that she may not have enough to care for her own future needs if this pattern continued. We encouraged her to visit facilities in her area and helped her to project the cost of a complex that she liked. We held a family meeting to discuss her options, including staying where she was and entering a nursing home, if it became necessary. This solution was not acceptable to her family because they wanted the benefit of time to choose the care they wanted her to have. While she clearly was not ready to move yet, she decided to put down a deposit and get on the waiting list of the home she preferred. It became obvious from our projections that she could not continue her gifting program and afford the move, so we started a five-year strategy to phase out the gifts. Had we not uncovered this transition and waited until she was ready to move, her financial situation may have eliminated this facility as an option.

Financial planning professionals do a good job of dealing with some transitions, a fair job with some others, and may totally neglect many other predictable circumstances. Retirement and college funding are examples of oft-discussed transitions. The inevitable transition of death gets plenty of dialogue, especially in insurance circles. However, issues like an aging parent who needs assisted living and the impact of that transition on your client's personal financial picture are often hit or miss. This is just the sort of transition that can throw someone's life into absolute chaos. Life takes unexpected turns, and in the process, nullifies our wishes and plans. We believe that we can do a better job of helping clients anticipate these life transitions and prevent a financial implosion and the destruction of dreams.

Mitch Anthony tells a story about a couple he knows:

Andrea and Tim are meticulous planners and disciplined savers. They developed a plan for retirement years ago and never swerved off course. Now, as Tim is retired and Andrea is fast approaching her target of selling her business, their financial plan has been rendered useless because of one unexpected turn in the life of Andrea's widowed father. Life happened, and, as it often does, leveled all rosy retirement hopes and good intentions in the process.

One night, as Andrea's aging father was walking in the night, he became disoriented and accidentally turned into the staircase and tumbled to the bottom. He was knocked unconscious. He lay in a heap for over 36 hours. Andrea and Tim had been away that weekend.

Andrea had called once with no answer, but figured her dad was out and about.

Andrea would soon learn that her father was having these disoriented episodes quite often but had not told her, as he didn't want to alarm or bother her. The prognosis was a long period of rehabilitation and the doctors recommended that she begin looking into an assisted-living facility. Some lifestyle and financial realities began to settle soon after visiting the first facility. Andrea and Tim were stunned by the costs. To put her father in a decent facility in close proximity would require that they subsidize the cost to the tune of $1,500 per month. This fact, combined with the sobering adjustment of Tim's premature retirement (downsized) just six months ago, left them adrift in a sea of confusion and financial backlash. Tim was doing sparse work for meager wages, netting out to an $1,800 per month reduction in household income. Andrea's business began to struggle, as she had to focus most of her attention on her father's situation. Each day she ignored her business worked toward depreciating the price she would be able to garner for it when she eventually sold it. These factors, combined with the subsidy for her father's new residence, resulted in a financial reversal of nearly $4,500 each month. No small challenge at any stage of life—much less at 66 and 61 years of age.

While the exact timing and specific nature of this event was not predictable, the fact that it was a real possibility was, and asking our clients to think about these potential disruptions to their lives is an integral part of the financial life planning process.

BENEVOLENCE SURVEY

While we will not cover the topic of charitable giving in depth when we review this questionnaire, we want to get some preliminary feedback from our clients about how they feel about giving (time or money). It has been our experience that one cannot always discover these tendencies by just looking at tax returns. Many of our clients would like to do much more than they are currently doing, but feel constrained because they believe they do not have enough money to make a difference. The dialogue that begins with the discussion to their answers to the questions on this form often reveals goals that, without further probing, may not be discovered. We will revisit this topic at another time.

THE POWER OF ASKING QUESTIONS

Peter had just retired from a successful career when he and Marsha first came to see us. Understanding clients' histories is an important part of the financial life planning process, and one of the first questions we asked Marsha was to describe her life as a child. She told us that her family had very little money when she was growing up, and that they literally did not know where their next meal was coming from. Her husband, Peter, had a much different childhood. His parents, while not wealthy, could probably be labeled as "upper middle class." Peter felt no need for very much that his parents could not afford. He later became a successful executive and inherited money from his parents, so when Marsha married Peter, her life was much different from the life she knew growing up. When I questioned them about their goals and desires, I discovered that Peter loved skiing and wanted to purchase a second home in Colorado. Most of their vacations were to ski resorts and, now that Peter was retired, he was planning more ski trips. Marsha traveled with him, but did not ski.

When we focused our attention on her goals, she first told us that she had no goals, and that whatever Peter wanted was fine with her. As we continued the process, she finally revealed that she hated those skiing trips, and would have preferred visiting her children in Arizona. She also confessed that she was upset about the prospect of owning a home in Colorado, which would have meant even more skiing trips. Peter was taken completely by surprise by these revelations, because he had no idea that Marsha felt this way. When they returned for our next meeting, they told us that they discussed Marsha's concerns and decided that Peter would continue to ski, but Marsha would visit the children in Arizona when he did so. I asked Marsha why she had not shared this with Peter before this time, and she replied, "No one ever asked before." There is power in asking the right questions. Since we label this important part of the process "discovery," doesn't that imply that we do more than ask someone to fill out a form?

YOUR CLIENTS' HISTORIES

One never knows which questions we ask will help us to discover behavior patterns that may be sabotaging a client's financial success. Rick Kahler, CFP®, tells about one of his clients (we'll call him Al), a successful person in his early thirties who was earning over $250,000 annually. Al's goal was to retire at 50. Since his annual budget specified that he was only spending $60,000, Rick's paraplanner told him that Al would have no problem retiring at 50. There was one major problem, however. In spite of the fact that Al had been earning this money for several years, the only money he managed to save was a small amount in his 401(k) plan. When Rick pointed out this obvious discrepancy, Al told Rick that he bought furniture one year, took an expensive vacation another year. He always seemed to find some way to spend all of the money he earned.

I suppose Rick could have accepted this, but Rick is a financial life planner and takes the time to understand his clients' histories and attitudes before making recommendations. He asked his client about his money history. Al responded, "As a young man, I was the only one in the family that was able to save money. I opened a bank account and accumulated $8,000. I was only 22 and was not earning very much at the time. I was so proud of my accomplishment that I boasted to my family about it. Shortly after that, I got a call from my sister, who was in trouble with the law and needed an attorney. She asked for the money I had saved to help her. The rest of my family interceded on her behalf and told me that my sister might go to prison if I didn't help. So I had to use all of the money I saved to pay for my sister's legal fees."

Rick was quietly listening. He recounts what happened next. "Al stopped talking for a moment and a look of revelation appeared on his face. It was obvious that he had just discovered something that was important. 'Rick,' he said, 'I have just realized that I have not saved another dollar since then, because if I have nothing and a family member calls for help, I can simply say that I don't have it.'" "I just sat there, stunned," Rick said. "He discovered for the first time at that meeting the reason he had not been saving." Rick went on to demonstrate to Al that it would be impossible for him to reach his goal of early retirement unless he committed to saving money. Al's knowledge of why he was overspending was revealed to him because Rick asked the right questions and probed his history. As a result, Al started a regular investing program and his goal of retiring early is within reach. How many planners find that, in spite of all the quantitative evidence they offer, some clients continue on the same course of self-destruction? The answer to helping these people may be in understanding their histories.

That's the way it was with Jim, who became a client before we began asking questions about money history and attitudes. He was questioning each decision the firm was making with his investments. These questions went far beyond the normal and healthy inquiries that are a part of the educational process with most clients. It appeared to us that trust was a major issue for him, so I asked Jim for his permission to ask about his history and attitudes about money. Jim's first memory of money was of his grandmother who, on her visits to his home, would sit him on her lap and produce a bag full of coins. He was quite young at the time and did not know the values of the various coins. She would pull a dime and a penny from the bag and ask, "Would you like the larger, shiny, orange coin or the small silver one?" Her voice inflection clearly communicated to him that the penny was more valuable and, of course, that is exactly what he would choose. It was not until later that he discovered that (in his words), "She was taking advantage of my naïveté and cheating me." He also recounted a situation when he was ready to enter graduate school and his father, because of a disagreement they were having at the time, informed him that he would not be paying his tuition. Money was being used as a weapon!

As Jim related these stories about his life, you could see an understanding of his behavior becoming very clear to him. He told us that he always had difficulty trusting anyone when it came to money, but that he never associated his lack of trust with these events in his life. He apologized for questioning our motives because intellectually, he knew that we were interested in his welfare. He acknowledged that his actions may have been sabotaging his relationship with his financial planner and asked us to be patient with him. Before he left that day, I jokingly asked him if, the next time he questioned our decisions, it would be okay to remind him "I am not your grandmother." He chuckled, and replied, "Of course." Does he occasionally question some of our decisions? Yes, but the relationship is no longer in jeopardy.

What do these stories have in common? When these clients were asked in-depth questions about their histories, they made their own discoveries about their lives and what was important to them. The above stories are only representations of what we can do to improve the quality of our clients' lives if we take the time to go beyond asking superficial questions, such as "When do you want to retire?" In order for us to be more effective in helping our clients achieve their goals in life, we need to have as much information about them as they are willing to share. And since we all know that our attitudes and behaviors about money are shaped by our life experiences, the discovery process needs to include questions about their money history. How, for example, could you do tax planning for your clients by simply asking them how much they paid in taxes last year without actually looking at their tax returns? Good quantitative data gathering needs to look beneath what our clients may be representing their financial conditions to be. Likewise, qualitative discovery requires that we ask questions that will help us to understand our clients and what is significant to them.

Another method of learning about your clients' histories, including their attitudes about money, is to ask a more general open-ended question. Elissa Buie, CFP®, asks all of her new clients to recount their life histories:

> Several years ago, I hired a business consultant who wanted me to identify my target market. He asked me to examine my clients to find a common thread among my best clients. I started by listing the people I liked working with and cross-referenced them to the ones that were most profitable. I wasn't surprised to discover that many of my clients appeared on both lists. I wanted to understand what similarities they had, and found none—except for one thing. They were the clients I knew the best—the ones with whom I had the most intimate relationships. I told my consultant this, and he said, 'Elissa, we can't build a marketing plan that targets people you know well!' That was obvious, but I wanted to find a way to jump-start what normally took five years to develop. I knew that after working with clients for several years, they would share their stories and life dreams with me. I felt that knowing a person's life history would be a good place to start. We ask all of our new clients, 'Tell us about yourself, we'd like to know your life history.' An open-ended question like this enables them to go where they want to go with the answer. What they talk about is our first clue to what really matters in their lives. What I did not realize at the time was that there is such a huge intimacy in being asked and actually being listened to.

VALUES AND ATTITUDES

Ayn Rand has written, "Happiness is that state of consciousness which proceeds from the achievement of one's values." Therefore, the interview questions listed below ask our clients about their values as well as their history. People come to us to help them make good financial decisions. We all know how disconnected we feel when our actions in life are not aligned with our core values. Knowing what our clients value most in life will provide us with the information to guide them in the right direction. Roy Disney wrote, "It's not hard to make decisions when you know what your values are." As Olivia Mellon, Ph.D., author and psychologist, says, "If your relationship with money is not in balance, no amount of money will help you. It is your job (as financial planners) to help your clients find balance around money."

Our next step in the discovery process is to ask each spouse the interview questions shown below, while the other remains silent. Bill Bachrach suggests that you ask, "Which one of you would like to go first?" and begin with the other spouse. When the dominant spouse answers first, his/her answers could affect how the other spouse responds. I have used this technique and found it to be quite effective. We also find it helpful to have an associate planner at the meeting taking notes so the interviewer remains totally engaged with the clients. The questions:

1. Tell me about your family when you were growing up.
2. Was money discussed at the dinner table?
3. What messages, direct or indirect, did you receive from your mother regarding money?
4. What messages did you receive from your father?

5. Describe your parents' financial histories.
6. What financial values and/or discussions with your parents continue to affect you today?
7. What is your first memory about money?
8. What was learned from that experience?
9. Describe a painful memory about money.
10. Describe a joyful memory about money.
11. Describe your work history.
12. What were some of the financial decisions you have made in the past that you regret?
13. What were some of the best financial decisions you made in the past?
14. What are your major beliefs about money?
15. What are your positive feelings about money?
16. What are your negative feelings about money?
17. What do you do to deal with these feelings?
18. How satisfied are you with the way you are dealing with these feelings?
19. What does financial independence mean to you?
20. How do you feel about passing assets to your heirs?
21. What part does philanthropy and charitable giving play in your value system?
22. What would be a desired outcome over the course of these initial meetings?
23. During our review three years from now, what will need to have happened between now and then for you to feel satisfied with your progress?

We never know when we will discover issues that are meaningful to our clients. While they most likely will occur in some of the other exercises that follow, we often uncover concerns that result in actions during this initial dialogue about their histories, attitudes, and values. Such was the case with Angela. She recounted the time in her life when she felt pain about money. Her family struggled financially and found it difficult to pay her tuition at the parochial school she attended. Almost every year she was called to the office and reminded that her tuition had not been paid and that she would be unable to complete the term if her parents did not pay what they owed. Humiliated, she would beg her parents to find some way to spare her this annual embarrassment. While they always managed to avoid their daughter's being asked to leave the school, the scene was replayed almost every year.

As Angela told her story, she hesitated, and I could she that she was pondering something. Finally, she told us that reliving that pain caused her to realize that she would like to do all she could to prevent other students from experiencing similar humiliation. Angela asked if it would be financially feasible to start a giving program to help to pay tuition for needy students at the high school from which she graduated. When we completed our quantitative analysis, we discovered that she had more than enough money to make a difference in the lives of about ten students each year. Psychologists tell us that the happiest people in the world are those who give—observing Angela certainly confirmed that for me. And we discovered this goal to help others simply because we asked a question about pain and money. We never know what part of the process will uncover heretofore hidden goals and desires, so we ask all of the questions to all of our clients all of the time.

Helen and Larry were successful executives when they first came to see us. When we asked about her history, Helen revealed that her father was a minister of a church in an upper-class neighborhood. Therefore, they lived among people who were considerably wealthier than they were. She recalls one neighbor who seemed to be very unhappy. She always seemed to be buying more things to satisfy herself, but it didn't help. The more she bought, the more she felt the need to buy. In addition, like addicts, these quick fixes did not last long and the cycle of buying would start again. Helen came away from that experience with the notion that money not only cannot buy happiness, it may actually help to elude it. Her neighbors seem so obsessed with spending their money for gratification that they ignored the things in life that really mattered.

As an adult, she managed to reach a high-level position with a large public company and was on her way to accumulating wealth, but she felt uncomfortable. Something was missing in her life, she believed, but she did not know what it was. Then 9/11 came. She worked in New York and had a relative who worked in the World Trade Center. On that day, when most people were evacuating the city, she made her way as close to the scene as she could, to seek information about her relative. When she got there and informed one of the people at the scene about the floor where he worked, she was told, "There is no way anyone on that floor survived"

A year later, she and her husband became clients of our firm and began the discovery process. As she communicated her childhood and 9/11 experiences, she realized that she needed to drastically change her life. Her job provided her with no rewards other than the money she earned. She told us she always knew that seeking money could become addictive and get in the way of a satisfying life, but she had done nothing about changing the pattern. However, she decided that day that things would change. We worked together on a plan to do that, and today, she and her husband are living in Arizona. She is working as a massage therapist and he has become a partner in a golf farm. At a recent visit, she told me that she has never been happier. It took an event like 9/11 and the recollection of her childhood experiences to help her to realize that her life needed to take a different direction.

As Galileo wrote, "All truths are easy to understand once they are discovered; the point is to discover them." Asking the right questions is a good place to start.

CHAPTER 4 SUMMARY

- Begin the dialogue by reviewing clients' answers to the preliminary questionnaires.
- Ask about the future—not retirement.
- Help them to discover what is important to them.
- Uncover current and future transitions.
- Ask about your clients' attitudes about charitable giving.
- Be a biographer—ask about your clients' histories.
- Discover your clients' values and attitudes about money.

ENDNOTES

1. Ross Levin, (2001) "Pseudogenes," *Journal of Financial Planning,* November 2001, p.28

5 Understanding Your Clients' Goals

*Understanding human needs is half
the job of meeting them.*

—Adlai Stevenson

"We want to retire when we are 55." That is what
George and Joan told us was their primary goal the
first time we met. They were each 45 at the time,
saving for retirement, and well on their way toward
accomplishing that goal. In addition to being married,
they were partners in a successful clinical psychology
practice. While their incomes were substantial, the
amount of money they were saving for retirement
and their children's education produced a lifestyle
that did not reflect the resources they had.

I could have accepted that goal without further
probing, but it is my experience that many clients do
not articulate what is most important to them at a
get-acquainted meeting. When they returned for
their first meeting as clients, we used the process
outlined in this book. As we completed the exercises

and asked our questions, several other goals became evident. Most notably, they said that they always dreamed of owning a beach home. When they talked about this goal, they became very animated. It was apparent to me that this was something they both really wanted. When I asked what had stopped them from doing it, they said they never could find the money to "take the plunge." Another discovery we made during the process was that they thoroughly enjoyed practicing psychology. This certainly did not seem to align with their goal of retiring early, so I followed up by asking additional questions such as:

- What is it that you want to retire from in ten years?
- What, if anything, are you going to retire to?
- If you enjoy your practice so much today, why would that change in ten years?
- What will you do with your time when you are retired?
- What would be more important to you—owning a beach home or retiring at age 55?

The answers to these and other questions revealed to me—and, more importantly, to them—that they would very likely miss their practice. At one point, they actually said, "We can't imagine not practicing psychology, even if it would be part-time." Moreover, our long-term projections demonstrated that it would be financially risky to purchase a beach home and retire at the age they originally planned. So, I asked the critical question: "Are you willing to sacrifice your goal of owning a beach home in order to retire at age 55?" The prospect of never owning a beach home (a probable outcome if they retired at 55) was something they were unwilling to accept.

Two years later, they called to tell me that they had found the beach home of their dreams. In all of the time I have known them, I never heard them as excited and enthusiastic as they were that day. We liquidated part of the portfolio for a down payment on the beach home. They also agreed to reduce the money they were investing each month by $3,000 until their children completed college. They were very willing to delay their retirement from 55 to 60—or even later—to enhance their lifestyle now and in the future. "After all," they said, "we do love what we are doing." If I had accepted their originally stated goals without exploring any further, they would have probably continued saving and sacrificing for a future that they did not really want. This reminds me of what that great American philosopher, Yogi Berra, said, "If you don't know where you're going, you might not get there."

GETTING AT THE HEART OF WHAT YOUR CLIENTS REALLY WANT

So why did George and Joan have a goal of early retirement in the first place? Could it be that society (as well as many financial advisers) sends the message that depriving ourselves today in order to retire early is the financially prudent thing to do? Why is it that so many planners make retirement a financial goal rather than the life decision that it really is? At a recent meeting, a financial planner approached me and asked me when I was going to retire. "With all due respect," I replied, "why would I want to stop doing something that I love to do?" She didn't seem to have an answer. If it is our job to improve the quality of our clients' lives (and I do believe that financial planning done well does just that), then we need to stop asking presumptuous questions such as, "When do you plan to retire?" As we mentioned earlier, a better way to discover what they want in life is to ask, "How do you visualize your life when you are in your sixties, seventies, and eighties?" This encourages clients to focus on their lifestyles and activities rather than a predetermined date when they need to stop working.

A financial planner once told me that it was arrogant to believe that many clients don't really know what their goals are. We suppose that means that we must accept everything clients say as accurate representations of what they want in their lives, as well as disregard those who have said, "I didn't really know what I wanted then—just what I thought I wanted." Moreover, Olivia Mellon, Ph.D., tells us that it is rare for clients to verbalize what is really important to them if we simply ask, "What are your goals?"

We assume that clients consciously know what they want. Often, they don't. They have to discover it. Remember John, who owned the used parts business that he was going to sell to one of his employees? He discovered through questioning that he didn't want to retire—what he really wanted to do was reorganize his business. The psychologists whose story was recounted at the beginning of this chapter seemed so clear and resolute about their goal of early retirement, yet they discovered that other goals were more important to them.

Nothing we do for clients is more important than uncovering and prioritizing their goals—not if we consistently want to get the boat in the right slip!

ADDING VALUE THROUGH DISCOVERY

Dan Wheeler, of Dimensional Fund Advisers, wrote, "Unless you understand where clients are today and where they want to be down the road, you cannot add value to their lives." And simply asking them to list their goals does not get the job done. About 20 years ago, I decided to purchase a vacation home at the New Jersey shore. I had always enjoyed being near the ocean and was excited at the prospect of having a place to go on weekends. I narrowed my choices to two houses. One was a two-bedroom condo on the beach and the other was a duplex, which was either a long walk or a short drive to the beach. The costs were similar, but the duplex offered the financial benefit of rental income from the unit I would not be occupying. After much consideration, I purchased the duplex.

I wasn't in my new home for very long before I realized that being a landlord was not what I had in mind when I decided to buy a shore home. I was interested in a place to relax on weekends. However, my tenants were loud and often late with their rent. At the end of their lease, the realtor who was managing the property had to find new tenants. That took several months. The new tenants damaged the property and their security deposit did not cover the expenses needed for repairs. Since most of these properties were owned by investors and not owner-occupied as mine was, the neighborhood began to deteriorate. You get the idea. I wanted a respite to enjoy on summer weekends and, instead of that, bought into tension. That certainly was not what I was looking for when I bought the property.

Clearly, I made a mistake when I purchased the duplex instead of the condo. I made a financial decision instead of a quality-of-life decision. What if I were the client of a financial life planner at that time, and she asked the same questions of me that I now ask all of my clients? She would have wanted to know my purpose for buying the home.

When she discovered that I wanted it for spending relaxing weekends at the beach, she would have reminded me that the condo was clearly a better life choice. If you could afford either, she may have asked, why not opt for the home that has the best opportunity of satisfying your goal? In all probability, I would have bought the condo and been happier.

We all need someone else to dialogue with before making major decisions. I was not buying the property for financial purposes, and a good financial life planner would have reminded me of that. Ironically, because the neighborhood had suffered the problems I mentioned, when I finally sold the duplex, it was for $30,000 less than I paid for it! The condos, by the way, were selling for $50,000 over their original price. So it actually turned out to be a poor financial decision as well. If a quantitative planner had asked me to list my goals, I would have written that I wanted a home at the shore. He, no doubt, would have followed up with, "How much will it cost?" After the projections, he would have informed me that I could afford the home and believed that his job was done. And he would have gotten it wrong, because he didn't ask enough questions to understand my motivation. *Wrong boat slip again!*

In the initial get-acquainted interview, prospective clients usually communicate their general goals to us, but they reveal far more to us when we take them through our goal-setting meeting(s). Over the years, we have discovered that most clients do not discuss many of their wishes and desires when we ask the simple question, "What are your goals?" In order to get beyond, "I want to retire and educate my children," we need a process that helps our clients discover and communicate what is most important in their lives. For our firm, the initial goal-setting process consists of four steps:

1. Asking them to answer three questions posed by George Kinder in his "Seven Stages of Money Maturity" workshops (see discussion below)
2. Identifying their goals
3. Prioritizing their goals
4. Determining the price for accomplishing their goals

THE THREE QUESTIONS

We owe a great deal to George Kinder, who developed these questions and uses them in his workshop. I was first exposed to them when I attended his seminar in 2000. They have had a profound effect on me personally. Moreover, their use with our clients has been invaluable in helping to discover what really matters in their lives. The answers to these questions are the foundation for the rest of our goal-setting process.

- **All the Money You Need.** We open this part of the process by telling our clients that we would like each of them to write their answers to three questions. Without revealing the other two questions, we present each client with a sheet of lined paper with the following question on the top: *"Imagine that you have all of the money you will ever need now and in the future. What will you do with it? How will you live your life? What will change?"* We have chosen to add at the bottom of this and the other two pages the following phrase: "Your responses will not be shared with anyone and will remain confidential unless you choose to discuss them openly. It is entirely up to

77

you." These exercises are meant to help our clients look at their lives and determine what they want the future to look like, and we believe that they need to feel safe to write anything they want. In reality, only one client chose not to share, but that confirmed for us that we should not force any of them to do so. With their permission, we discuss their answers before presenting them with the next question.

The first question is powerful because so many clients put unnecessary constraints on their ability to reach their goals. They simply doubt that they have the money to do some of the things they want to do. They are so unattainable, they believe, that they just choose not to share these dreams with us. It has been our experience (and I suspect yours) that most clients are so afraid of not having enough money to do the things they consider necessary that they do not dare to dream. This question gives them the opportunity to dream. The results are often remarkable.

Ralph, who owned a successful business, chose to share his answer with us. As he began to talk about what he had written, he became very emotional. "I have always wanted to help children who are less fortunate than I, but I just don't have enough money to make a difference. If I had all of the money I needed, I would use part of it to establish a scholarship fund for kids who cannot afford to go to college. I have thought about this a great deal, but I am realistic. There is no way I can do it without sacrificing my family's goals for the future." "What if you had enough money, what would you do?" I asked. "Why even discuss it? It would be impossible," he replied. When I pressed him for an answer, he told me that, ideally, he would fund an endowment for $500,000 at his alma mater and stipulate that the money be used to fund educations for needy students. "I can visualize having an annual dinner where I would invite all of the students whose lives I have affected." He really became emotional as he described what living this dream would be like for him.

Ralph did not know it at that time, but he clearly had enough to do exactly what he wanted to do. When we did our projections at a future meeting, we illustrated that gifting $100,000 per year for five years would have no effect on the other goals he wanted to accomplish. He has pledged $500,000 in $100,000 installments to fulfill a dream he never thought was possible. If we had done the normal quantitative data gathering, we would have never discovered this hidden desire Ralph had. There were no clues to be found anywhere. His tax return did not reveal that he was very charitably inclined. Up to the time of our meeting, he had not even shared this goal with his wife. He saw no reason to, since he was certain he could not afford it. If we want our clients to reveal what is most important to them in their lives, we need to remove any artificial constraints they may have put on their ability to do what they want. This question does the job.

- **Five Years to Live.** When they are finished writing their answers and sharing their responses (if they so chose), we proceed to the second question: "*You have just come from a visit to your doctor who told you that you have only five to seven years to live. The good part is that you won't ever feel sick. The bad part is that you will have no notice of the moment of your death. As you let the emotional impact of the situation sink in, ask yourself these questions: How will I change my life? What will I choose to do in the amount of time I have remaining?*"

Many of us know people who came close to death and completely changed their lives. The near-death experience caused them to evaluate what was most important in their lives. Of course, we all know that we will die; we just don't know when. So why do so many of us need the shock of coming face to face with death to do what really matters to us? We are so caught up in our lives that many of us may be forgetting to live. Since none of us knows how long we have, why aren't we doing what is important to us now? Do we need to wait until someone presents us with a death sentence? While some of our clients write that they would change nothing, most would do some of the things they always promised themselves they would do but never got around to. For some, it may involve travel, for others, spending more time with their families, and for some, a change in careers.

When Mary and Mark discussed what each had written, we discovered that they both wanted to take a trip throughout Europe with their children and grandchildren. While they had discussed this often and always put it off, they agreed that they would no longer delay this trip. Their "assignment" for our next meeting was to go to their travel agent to determine what it would cost so we could plan for the expenditure. A year later, they made the trip of a lifetime. They sent me a card from Prague that said, "We never would have done this if it weren't for you." Forgive the redundancy, but there is power in asking the right questions.

• **One Day Left.** The third and final question: *"The doctor told you this time that you have only one day left in your life. Ask yourself, what am I feeling? What are my regrets and longings? What dreams will be left unfulfilled? What do I* *wish I had done? What do I wish I had been?"* As you might surmise, this is the most emotionally charged question, and often the most revealing for what is most important to them. Our goal is to try to accomplish those wishes so that, if asked that question again, their response would be, "I would change nothing." Some of our clients actually write that answer, and it is gratifying to them and us to hear them share that. However, more people than not have unfulfilled dreams.

Ruth was not one of our clients. She was employed in the financial planning profession, but not as a planner. At an industry meeting, she approached me and said, "I wanted to tell you, Roy, that you have changed my life." I was taken completely by surprise by this statement since our only contact was very casual at an occasional meeting, so I asked what I could have possibly done to affect her life. "I heard you speak about a year ago," she said, "and you told the audience about those three questions you ask every client. I was so impressed by them that I decided to have my husband and I write our answers when I got home. You probably don't know this, Roy, but my husband is an architect. He wrote that his biggest regret in life was that he had never built a home for us. We bought a lot and our new home is being built as we speak. The next time you are in our city, I would like you to visit the home you helped us build."

IDENTIFYING GOALS

Answering these questions sets the groundwork for establishing goals. While what is most important to them is fresh in their minds, we ask each of them to independently list their goals and classify each as a "core value," an "ought to" or a "fun to" (see Exhibit 1—"Life Goals"). For example, a client may list "funding my children's education" as a core value "giving more money to charity" as something they ought to do, and "buying a boat" as fun to do. It is also important for our clients to understand the difference between a goal and a tactic. We tell them, for example, that increasing the return on their portfolio is not a goal, but may be a method to accomplish another goal, such as funding their children's educations.

It is important that this be an open-ended exercise and we do not provide them with a checklist of typical goals. We want them to flesh out whatever comes to their minds. The last thing we want to do is suggest goals that they should have. It has been our experience, having used both tactics, that the open-ended approach is the best method to uncover what means the most to our clients. To illustrate this point, try this experiment with two people you know. Provide one with a blank sheet of paper and ask her to write her goals for life. Give the other a list to check off the goals he wants to accomplish. Keep the answers, and one week later ask each to recall the life goals they listed. What people value most in their lives and have written in their own words will not be forgotten. While it is likely that these goals will also appear on the checklist, other items that they checked off simply because they were an option may obscure their most important goals. Moreover, they are much more likely to take ownership of goals they have written in their own words. As you can see, the form we give them (Exhibit 1) lists only the general categories. The rest is up to them. We want to know what it is that they want to accomplish more than anything else. If a goal does not come up for them at this time, it is probably not a very high priority.

We suggest that you do all of these exercises yourself. Write your answers to the three questions and immediately thereafter, list the goals that are important in your life. You may be surprised at what comes up for you. I do not ever remember a time when the goals my clients shared with me during our initial consultation were the same as what emerges at this time. Those goals may still be present, but new ones seem to always surface. If you believe that your first duty as a financial planner is to discover the critical issues your clients have, you need to ask thought-provoking questions. Remember, nothing is more powerful than helping people get where they want to go. Of course, that assumes that you know where that is. This and the previous exercise will help you to discover it.

PRIORITIZING AND CLARIFYING GOALS

The next step in the process is relatively straightforward, and is something that most planners do. This is the first time that you will merge the goals of each partner on one sheet. Note the similarities and needs to reconcile any differences they may have. Of course, many of the differences may be non-competing goals (he wants to play more golf and she wants to join a gym), and these are easy to deal with. Some may be more difficult to resolve. Suppose, for example, that one of them wants to buy a vacation home at the beach and the other would rather use the money to travel. As we discussed in the Introduction, we are not marriage counselors, and they may need to deal with this issue on their own. However, we certainly don't ignore it—we ask them if they want us to illustrate the financial impact of each. In any event, as we continue to meet in the future, we will ask them if they have reconciled the second home issue.

We transcribe each goal from the previous form to the Prioritizing & Clarifying Goals form (see Exhibit 2). Once again, dialogue is the key. It is important that we understand the motivations behind these goals. Remember the mistake I made when I bought the duplex because I had no one to remind me of my motivation for buying a shore home. Therefore, we discuss each goal with our clients before assigning a priority code (from 5—a must, to 1—not that important). A target date and an estimated cost for all goals are projected and listed. This gives us most of the information we need to do preliminary projections. Depending on the clients, it often takes more than one meeting to complete the goal-setting process. We may ask them to complete the Life Goals form at home and bring it to our next meeting. Putting a time constraint on this important part of the process may risk not getting it right. How long does it take? What if you were washing a dirty jar with soap and water and wanted to ensure that it was clean and free from any soap residue? How many times must you rinse the bottle before it is clean? Five? Ten? Twenty? The answer is simple—*until it is clean!* And so it is with goal setting for your clients. You continue until you get it right! Because getting it right is what we are paid to do. And getting it right will give you the satisfaction of having done a good job. But most important, getting it right will help you clients improve the quality of their lives.

CHAPTER 5 SUMMARY

- Don't assume that your clients consciously know what they want.
- Nothing we do for our clients is more important than uncovering and prioritizing their goals.

- We add value through discovery.
- Most people need others with whom to dialogue before making major decisions.
- Before asking your clients for their goals, have them answer the three "Kinder questions."
- Use open-ended exercises—not checklists—when asking clients to list their goals.
- Prioritize and estimate the cost of accomplishing each goal.
- Do the exercises yourself.

Financial Planning: The Next Step

EXHIBIT 1:

Life Goals

NAME_____   DATE_____

For each goal, please select the appropriate priority and time frame.

Priority Code: **H** = High   **M** = Medium   **L** = Low
Time Frame: **C** = Current   **N** = Near Term (1–5 years)   **L** = Long Term (Over 5 years)

FAMILY	Priority	Time Frame
WORK/CAREER		
FINANCIAL		
PERSONAL GROWTH		

EXHIBIT 1 *(CONTINUED)*:

Life Goals (2)

NAME_____   DATE_____

For each goal, please select the appropriate priority and time frame.

Priority Code: **H** = High   **M** = Medium   **L** = Low
Time Frame: **C** = Current   **N** = Near Term (1–5 years)   **L** = Long Term (Over 5 years)

LEISURE/RECREATION	Priority	Time Frame
COMMUNITY		
CHARITABLE		
LEGACY		

EXHIBIT 2:

Prioritizing & Clarifying Goals			

Name _____ Date: _____

Goals	Priority Code*	Date to Complete	Cost to Complete

Priority Code:

A. Extremely important   C. Moderately important
B. Important   D. It would be nice but not necessary

6 | *Numbers Matter*

The vision must be followed by the venture.
It is not enough to stare up the steps—
we must step up the stairs.

—Vance Havner

"Oo-oh dream weaver, I believe you can get me through the ni-ight; Oo-oh dream weaver, I believe we can reach the morning li-ight…" We may not be dream weavers as the song by Gary Wright declares, but financial life planners are *dream facilitators.* In previous chapters, we demonstrated a system that will help your clients discover and communicate to you the goals and dreams that are important in their lives.

Lest we forget that it takes technical expertise and good quantitative information to get our boats into the right boat slips with no damage, this chapter will outline the steps we need to take to help our clients implement their goals. Most of what we have covered in prior chapters has dealt with interior discovery because this is the area for which most financial planners have not been trained. The analogy about docking a boat, however, made it clear that planners need to strike a balance between discovering what our clients want in their lives and implementing technical expertise. We devote only one chapter to this important part of the process for two reasons. First, the training most of us receive concentrates on quantitative issues and we do not need to be redundant. Also, this is not a book about technical expertise. It is about discovering what is important to your clients and showing them how to get there.

CASH FLOW PROJECTIONS

It does seem appropriate, however, to discuss some of the things we do with the numbers (without getting into technical strategies) to help our clients implement their dreams and goals. Mostly, it involves demonstrating with long-term cash flow projections what it is possible for them to accomplish without the risk of running out of money. Our firm prefers using cash flow driven software that includes Monte Carlo simulations. These programs give us the greatest flexibility to model future expenses, including sporadic and one-time expenditures. Moreover, since income taxes can have a profound effect on future cash flow, we need a software program that calculates state and federal taxes (based on current laws) for each year of our projections. Simply using an average tax rate will not provide us with information that is accurate enough for us to feel comfortable making recommendations.

As financial life planners, we bristle at the notion that rules of thumb are actually relevant when we plan for our clients' futures. Have any of us really experienced clients who retire and immediately begin spending 75 percent of their pre-retirement income? Most of our clients who retire may actually spend more money in the early years of their retirement, and this fact needs to be accounted for in our long-term projections. When current expenditures are itemized, we can more accurately project what future spending may look like. For example, it may be logical to assume that some expenses (such as clothes) may decrease after retirement, but that others (such as travel) may increase. Also, using an average rate of inflation, such as 3 percent, does not recognize that some expenditures may increase by more than that. Health care is an expense that has consistently increased by more than the CPI. We are not in the "rule-of-thumb" business. It is our job to do our best to project the unique financial futures of each client.

MONTE CARLO SIMULATIONS

It is appropriate at this time to discuss the use of Monte Carlo analyses. As mentioned earlier, the purpose of this chapter is not to have a technical discussion of tools and strategies. Much has been written on these subjects, including the use and efficacy of Monte Carlo simulations. While we will acknowledge that using tools like these will not accurately predict the future, are there any programs that can do that? If nothing more, a Monte Carlo analysis demonstrates just that—the future is impossible to predict and will be affected by situations that are beyond our control. Moreover, the most unpredictable of scenarios is likely to be future invest-ment returns. While we know that this tool is not perfect, it certainly is superior to linear projections, no matter how conservative they may be. Until we discover a better method, we will continue to use Monte Carlo simulations to help our clients make decisions about their futures.

BASE PLAN

Our first step in the quantitative planning process is to project our clients' financial futures assuming that no major changes are made. This is labeled the "base plan." These projections will include core goals they may have, such as educating their children or retiring at a certain age. However, dreams, goals, and hopes that we uncovered during the discovery process and did not plan for are not included in these preliminary projections. We complete a Monte Carlo simulation for this base scenario to demonstrate the chances of success if they continue their current spending patterns. This is a good place to start, because our clients need to know how their current expenditures may affect their future financial security. Of course, if they are on a course that may result in an unsuccessful conclusion, we need to deal with that at this point. Dreams may need to be put on hold. Fortunately, most of our clients are not in this situation. Our experience is that it is far more likely that clients are under spending and avoiding additional expenditures for several reasons. Some may believe that spending more will put them at risk to run out of money. Others have been savers all of their lives and find it difficult to change from being savers to spenders, regardless of how much money they may have. Perhaps they heard messages from their parents about the Great Depression or other financial difficulties and believe that there is no such thing as too much money. And there are those who have just refused to let themselves dream. We hope that our discovery process helped them to discover some of those goals. This part of the process can make a financial life planner a dream facilitator.

SCENARIOS

For our purposes, we will use a fictitious client situation. Let us assume that we have done cash flow and future projections of their base plan and that our Monte Carlo analysis indicates that they have a 99 percent probability of success (we never illustrate 100 percent). Once we feel assured that they are not in danger of running out of money, our next steps would be to run the plan with other scenarios to test the probability of attaining each of their other goals. Suppose, in this case, the other goals we discovered during our process (listed in order of priority) were as follows:

1. Purchase a vacation home for $600,000
2. Contribute an additional $25,000 a year to charitable causes that are important to them
3. Take three major vacations at a cost of $25,000 each
4. Gift each of their two children and four grandchildren $22,000 a year

   Our first scenario would be to add the purchase of the vacation home. Doing so does not significantly change their long-term prognosis and the Monte Carlo simulation still indicates a success probability of 99 percent. We would continue with the next scenario, which was to contribute an additional $25,000 a year to charity. Since our hypothetical clients have significant assets, we also find this to be a very attainable goal and the chance of success continues to look very favorable (98 percent). We continue to illustrate the effects of each additional scenario, until we discover that gifting $132,000 each year to their children and grandchildren ($22,000 x 6) would reduce their chances of success to 72 percent. This is unacceptable to them, so we project how much they could give and maintain a success probability of 90 percent. We calculate that gifting a total of $30,000 a year should not create future problems.

If all of a client's goals are attainable, we may run scenarios that demonstrate the effects of spending additional money each year ($25,000, $50,000, etc.) until we have "pushed the envelope" too far. This systematic process lets our clients know how much they can reasonably spend in the future. Of course, we will revisit these and other goals during our regular reviews.

MESSAGES OUR CLIENTS HEAR

Most of our clients have been affected by messages they have heard from parents, financial advisers, the financial media, and others. These messages may cause some of them to limit their spending. Other clients may overspend, regardless of how much they have earned or accumulated. While we need to demonstrate the potential results of their current behavior, it is important that we understand that it takes more than cash flow projections to change behavior that it has taken a lifetime to learn. We hope that the interior discovery we have begun will be a first step for our clients who have these issues, but we need to understand that the process may take months or even years to make a difference. It is our job, as financial life planners, to be with them and guide them in the decisions they make about money.

Many of our clients may erroneously believe that they do not have enough resources to accomplish some of their dreams and goals, so they deprive themselves for no good reason. For these clients, we need to demonstrate the financial effects of doing what they want to do. Of course, if we don't ask the right questions, they may never tell us. Like the client who never shared his passion to provide college scholarships for needy students, they may truly believe that many of their dreams are impossible to attain, so they simply do not share them with us. The numbers do become powerful when they are used to show people what is possible in their lives.

CONNECTING WITH YOUR CLIENTS

As we have stressed in previous chapters, however, no matter how compelling the numbers may be, some people may not implement the steps they need to take to get what they say they want out of life. Richard and Rita were retired and had a net worth of over $12 million. Despite this fact, they did not have enough money to maintain their lifestyle for the rest of their lives. Only $3 million was liquid and they were spending over $350,000 a year. They were on a collision course and knew it, yet they seemed unwilling to implement the recommendations that would improve their financial condition. It was obvious that they needed to either reduce their spending or sell some of their assets. The Monte Carlo simulation demonstrated that their current course would have virtually no chance of success. Our initial discovery process did not reveal to them or to us why they were reluctant to change their ways.

The reality is that you cannot solve interior issues with exterior solutions.

At one of our meetings, I shared some personal information about my money life with them—issues I had discovered at George Kinder's workshop. When they returned for our next session, they told me that they decided to sell one of their homes and reduce their expenses by $50,000 a year. Their chances of success improved from 12 percent to 86 percent. When I asked what had made them change their minds and implement our recommendations, Richard answered, "At our last meeting when you shared your story with us, you became a human being. Rita and I discussed our situation when we got home and decided that it was in our best interests to follow your recommendations." One may not be able to predict what it takes to connect with your clients. I only know that doing so is essential if we are to be dream facilitators. Sharing my story was the catalyst for Richard and Rita.

Throughout this book, we have stressed the importance of discovery and the skills and tools necessary to understand your clients' goals. This chapter tells us that we cannot ignore the power of numbers in helping our clients implement strategies to achieve those goals. Our next chapter covers the value we bring to clients when we manage their assets.

CHAPTER 6 SUMMARY

- Long-range cash flow projections are essential to demonstrate the ability for your clients to meet their goals.
- Create a scenario for each of their goals and dreams.
- Rules of thumb are not appropriate for financial life planners.
- Monte Carlo simulations demonstrate the range of possible outcomes.
- It is important for your clients to understand how their money messages affect their ability to be financially healthy.
- We need to be patient and not expect our clients to change their behaviors after one or two meetings.
- Connecting with your clients will help your clients to implement your recommendations.
- Financial life planners are dream facilitators.

7 Moving Beyond the Investment Mentality: Is the Emperor Naked?

A child, however, who had no important job and could only see things as his eyes showed them to him, went up to the carriage. "The Emperor is naked," he said. ...everyone cried, "The boy is right! The Emperor is naked!" The Emperor realized that the people were right but could not admit to that.

—Hans Christian Andersen, adapted by Stephen Corrin in
Stories for Seven-Year-Olds. London 1964

When financial advisers promise clients consistently superior, above-market returns, are these promises as shallow and invisible as the clothes woven by the tailors in the Hans Christian Andersen fable? Are these advisers preying on the greed felt by many investors? If so, how long before the townspeople (average investors) discover that the emperor is naked? What will they do about it?

WHAT OUR CLIENTS ARE LOOKING FOR

Those of you who attended the FPA Retreat in Colorado Springs in 2004 were privileged to witness one of the most motivating sessions I have ever attended. Videotaped interviews with four clients of financial planners were presented, moderated by Susan Bradley of the Sudden Money Institute. Each client spoke of how important their relationship was with their planner and what it had meant to them. They recounted how the quality of their lives had improved. Some of the phrases and words they used to describe their experiences were "peace of mind," "trust," "friendship," "caring," "concern for our needs," "availability," and "competence." One could not help but notice two things all of these clients had in common: they treasured the relationship they had with their planners and *not one of them mentioned investments.*

I asked every adviser I interviewed for this book the following question: "How important is getting 'above-market' returns to your clients?" Not surprisingly, every one of them told me that it was not important to their clients. Reaching their goals was what was most important to them, regardless of what the markets might do. I do not mean to imply that investing our clients' money is something to be taken lightly or ignored. But to suggest that the main reason people hire us and retain our services is to obtain superior investment results may diminish what we really do for our clients. However, since this chapter is about investing, perhaps we should analyze what financial life planners really do for their clients when they manage their assets.

CONSTRUCTING PORTFOLIOS

One of the most important things we do for our clients is
to construct portfolios that are designed to meet their
individual goals. It is not the purpose of this chapter to
get into the technicalities of constructing investment
strategies. Enough has been written on that subject. We
all know that the basic purpose of any financial planning
system is to construct portfolios that represent the highest probabilities of achieving success for our clients. At
our firm, *we define success as meeting goals, not beating
markets.* Whether you use mutual funds, individual stocks,
separate accounts, or other vehicles, portfolios you design
for your clients should contain two very important com-
ponents. First, the expected returns, with some margins
for error, need to have a high probability for your clients
to achieve their long- and short-term goals. Second, the
strategy must be constructed in a way that it will not
cause your clients to abandon the policy when markets
are not doing well. Communicating realistic expectations
about the returns and volatility will be vital. Since I
believe that achieving above-market returns is something
that cannot be consistently delivered to clients, I tell
them that. Moreover, as financial life planners, we do not
need to beat the market to provide value to our clients.
And I'm talking about value for their investments, in addition to all of the other things we do for our clients.

WHAT IS YOUR ALPHA?

Dalbar Inc.'s 2003 update to the Quantitative Analysis of
Investor Behavior (QAIB) showed that investors looking for
superior returns often chased last year's winners and sold
other investments in their portfolios that had underperformed

for the previous year. They likely executed this strategy out of fear or greed. In spite of the fact that they continued to be disappointed by moving money into equities following market upswings and selling them when the market was not doing well, they continued these self-destructive activities. Of course the market timing these people were doing did not work for the overwhelming majority of them, and the result was poor returns relative to the overall market. According to Dalbar, the average equity investor earned 2.57 percent annually, while the S&P 500 index earned 12.22 percent annually for the 19 years studied (1984–2002).

So why do so many financial planners believe and communicate to their clients that getting returns superior to the market is the primary value they bring to the relationship? Dalbar has demonstrated that, when left on their own, average investors got returns that were almost 8.5 percent lower than the market! As advisers, you do not need to beat the S&P to deliver value to your clients. You provide discipline. You see to it that they do not overreact to market swings. You stop them from doing the things that average investors do that cause them to get returns that are 8.5 percent below the market. However, many advisers I talk to diminish the importance of this discipline and judge themselves on their ability to beat some index. They fear that clients will not pay their fees if they do not do so. They must provide "alpha." What is alpha for financial life planners and their clients? We all know the technical definition of the term, but I would define it differently for my clients.

First, if we look at what we do quantitatively, the return we provide should be better on a risk-adjusted basis than what they would have gotten if left on their

own—not a return that is above some arbitrary index.
That is very difficult to measure because we have no way
of knowing what their results would have been had they
not engaged our services. However, Dalbar has certainly
provided us with a clue of how well the average do-it-
yourself investor does. In fact, if the return of the equity
portion of the portfolios you managed for the period studied by Dalbar were 2 percent *below* the S&P, you would
have benefited the average client by over 6 percent. That
is your alpha in percentage terms!

However, if we stray from the technical definition of
alpha and define it as "value we provide for our clients,"
then the term takes on a much broader meaning and defines
who we are as financial planners and what we do for our
clients. Alpha, if we insist on a quantitative measure, could
be reaching or exceeding the client's financial goals. If a
client needs to obtain a return of 6 percent to reach every
financial goal she has in life and your portfolio returns 6.5
percent, have you not provided alpha? How about the
clients who use their time in pursuits that they value and
enjoy, rather than agonizing about their portfolios? Is that
not alpha? Is peace of mind alpha? One of our clients
managed his own portfolio for years (and did a good job),
but hired us so he could devote more time to his practice
and family. During the bear market of 2000–2003, he
called to tell us how happy he was that we were the ones
that needed to make the tough decisions about his investments and not him. If he was so inclined, he could have
told us that we were providing the only alpha that meant
anything to him.

Beating the S&P 500? Let the money managers live or
die with that bogey. Your alpha is the peace of mind your

clients experience because of the discipline you bring to the investment management process.

WHAT WE DO FOR OUR CLIENTS

Marty Kurtz, CFP®, summarized what he does at a client appreciation dinner as follows: "I do asset allocation and planning reviews for all of you. And, you are all invested in fairly the same way with different allocations. To be honest, you could probably find 20 other advisers within ten miles of us who could all do a good job in these areas. We do those things and try to do them well but that is not what I am all about. The real value I want to bring to you is to know what really matters to you and to be a part of that." Marty honestly tells his clients that the difference between him and other advisers is not the way he invests their assets, but the way he invests in their lives.

WHAT IS RISK?

We believe many advisers, and certainly most clients, confuse risk and volatility. To us, the greatest risk for our clients is to discover that they do not have enough assets to achieve their most important goals in life. Reaching the age of 85 and discovering that you have outlived the portfolio you designed 20 years earlier is, by far, the riskiest strategy that one could ever devise. An investor may believe that a portfolio with 100 percent of assets invested in intermediate bonds may be risk-averse, but it will have no probability of succeeding if that person needs to experience a return of 5 percent over inflation to maintain his lifestyle for the long run. If we define risk as "running out of money before you run out of life," it is our duty to point out that a strategy that appears to be conservative may be the most risky.

Recently, a new client who was retired told us that he wanted little or no volatility in his portfolio. His portfolio was with a major brokerage firm and his broker had followed his client's instructions and constructed a portfolio of bonds of various maturities and no equities. The client told us that he did not want any of his money invested in stocks because he could not handle the "risk" (he meant volatility). Our long-term projections demonstrated that he was on target to run out of money in 12 years. We asked him if this was a risk he was willing to take, or would he be willing to accept some fluctuations and years when the portfolio lost money in order to significantly increase his chances for success. His broker had taken the easy way and, in spite of the fact that he was withdrawing an unsustainable amount from a portfolio invested 100 percent in bonds, never bothered to tell the client. We did. The result was a balanced portfolio of 50 percent equities and 50 percent fixed income. Will he fret over fluctuations? In the short run, probably. Nevertheless, as financial planners it is our duty to help our clients achieve their goals. When faced with the prospect of either accepting more volatility or changing their goals, my experience is that clients always choose to accept portfolio fluctuation as a price they need to pay for getting what they want out of life. In my opinion, financial advisers place too much emphasis on "risk tolerance" when portfolios are being designed for clients, and in many cases sacrifice the long-term financial welfare of their clients.

We all know the Serenity prayer: "Grant me the serenity to accept the things I cannot change, the courage to change the things I can, and the wisdom to know the difference." Let us not fool our clients and ourselves by making claims that rival those made by the tailors in the

Andersen story. We do enough good without having to claim more than we can deliver.

CHAPTER 7 SUMMARY

- Satisfied clients seldom cite investment returns as a primary reason for their satisfaction.
- Beating a market index is not the value financial life planners provide for their clients.
- Constructing portfolios that are designed to help clients meet their short- and long-term goals is more important than beating the S&P.
- Among the unique benefits financial life planners offer their clients are:
  - Peace of mind
  - Discipline
  - Better returns than most clients would get on their own
- Risk should not be confused with volatility.
- The greatest risk people face is running out of money before they run out of life.

8 | *Estate Planning: How Do You Want to Be Remembered?*

It is up to us to live up to the legacy that was left for us, and to leave a legacy that is worthy of our children and of future generations.

—Christine Gregoire, governor of Washington

Imagine asking someone on his death bed how he would like to be remembered, and getting the response: "As a person who had an estate plan that saved taxes." However, when I attend estate planning sessions that are led by attorneys and other financial advisers, the dominant theme is saving taxes. According to these session leaders, that should be the overriding factor when advisers recommend estate planning strategies for their clients.

AVOID LAWYERS WHO DEFINE SAVING TAXES AS ESTATE PLANNING

When recommending estate planning attorneys to our clients, we look for professionals who are not only technically proficient, but who also understand the human nature of estate planning.

Recently, a law firm that we have used with good results sent an attorney to work with one of our clients. The lawyer we usually use in that firm was on a leave of absence, so they sent a replacement. Since it was the first time we worked together, I decided to have a brief meeting half an hour before the client was to arrive to make sure that we were on the same page. I told him that what I liked best about his colleague was the holistic approach he took, and that taxes didn't drive every recommendation that he made. He agreed that that was the best approach to take, so I described my client's situation to him.

This was not a complicated case. My client (we'll call him Alan) was a single father who had custody of his 12-year-old son. At our meeting, he told the lawyer that he wanted his assets to be placed in trust for the benefit of his son and that his two sisters should be co-trustees. Everything seemed to be moving along fine until the lawyer began to ask questions about what would happen to the money if neither Alan nor his son were alive. Alan told him that he would want his estate split evenly between his sisters. The attorney asked "What if one of your sisters dies, do you want her share to go to her children (*per stirpes*) or to your other sister?" Alan didn't need to think about this, and he answered that he would want his surviving sister to inherit the assets. "That's not a good idea," the lawyer responded. "Why," Alan asked. "Because your surviving sister may have an estate tax problem if she were to die with all of that money in addition to other assets she may have," the lawyer answered.

This was the holistic, non-tax-motivated advice that he promised he would give my client. Let's summarize his recommendation: *Leave your money to someone else just to save taxes. It would have no impact on your assets, or even on your sister's. But it may affect the money she may be able to leave her children—children you have already told me you do not care to have inherit your money!* What, I wondered, would he have advised if we did not have the brief meeting before the client arrived? An extreme example? Perhaps, but it actually happened and it illustrates the obsession many attorneys have with taxes when they do estate planning. Of course, I interceded on my client's behalf and, regardless of how remote the possibility was of these contingencies occurring, his estate plan reflected *his* desires and not the lawyer's tax-motivated strategy.

FOCUS ON THEIR GOALS—NOT THEIR TAX BILL

Financial planners are also quick to jump to tax-savings strategies before understanding what their clients' desires are. In June 2004, my son A.J. decided that he wanted to move to California, where he had once lived for three years and met his wife. He was a stockholder in our firm, so we had to buy his shares in accordance with our company's stock redemption plan. He joined a financial planning firm in Newport Beach. This, of course, was a blow to our business. Moreover, having A.J. and my three grandchildren 3,000 miles away was going to take a huge personal adjustment. At a national meeting, a planner who knew A.J. asked about him and I informed him of the move. Now, this planner could have asked how A.J and his family were adjusting to living on the West Coast. He could have asked me about how I was doing and what it was like to have my grandchildren so far away. Instead, he said, "I guess that messes up your estate plan." I was not even sure what he meant by that (my estate would increase because of the additional shares?). I only know that I would not want to be his client! Are we so well trained in the technical issues that we lose sight of the more important human side of planning?

While it is certainly our responsibility to discuss the tax effects of estate planning decisions our clients make, our first duty is to understand what their desires are, regardless of the tax consequences. Too many planners are quick to recommend credit shelter trusts, irrevocable life insurance trusts, and other tax-savings strategies before having an in-depth conversation about what is most important for their clients. An obvious example would be in the case of a second marriage. While it may be tax-efficient to take full advantage of the marital deduction and maximize the unified credit with a trust, many of our clients may want to leave the major portion of their estates to their children, even if it exceeds the unified credit. We need to be open to that scenario, and avoid proclaiming, as the attorney did in the story earlier in this chapter, "That may not be a good idea." Is it our responsibility to point out the tax implications of that decision? Of course. But to attempt to change their plans just to save taxes would be a classic case of the tail wagging the dog. I have asked many estate planning attorneys what they would do if the estate tax were repealed. Most have told me that their practices would suffer, if not die, because the basis of all planning was the avoidance of estate taxes. One lawyer, however, told me that it would liberate him to concentrate on what really matters to his clients. Taxes, he said, are too often the overriding factor in planning, and more planners need to focus on their clients' legacies. Amen!

UNDERSTAND THEIR MOTIVATION

Marcee Yager, CFP®, who practices in the San Francisco area, tells a story that clearly demonstrates that it often takes time to completely understand our clients' motives, and creativity to help them to get what they want, regardless of the tax effects. In this case, her clients, Joan and Dick, were recently married—both for the second time with children from their previous marriages. Joan had inherited a family trust and was wealthy, but Dick had little left from his divorce settlement. He earned his money by buying real estate, remodeling it, and selling it. When Marcee first asked him what he wanted, he told her that he wanted everything he owned to be in community property because he believed in the marriage partnership. So Marcee told him how that would work. Then he said, "Okay, but now my kids will get nothing." She suggested that he purchase life insurance for their benefit. He thought that was a good idea, until he objected to paying premiums just to ensure that his children would get money. She couldn't get him to articulate what the real issue was. On the one hand, he wanted everything in community property. On the other hand, he felt poor, because "what's his is hers and what's hers is hers." No matter how many plans were devised, he refused to sign off on any of them. It was becoming apparent to Marcee that something that he wasn't sharing was bothering him, so she stopped suggesting solutions and began to concentrate on his issues.

She said, "I need help. You are torn between two conflicting goals, and I need clarity about what is troubling you so I can make this work for you." After several meetings and much discussion, he told Marcee, "I feel so guilty for having gotten a divorce and so angry about the effects of that. Having to give my ex-wife so much of what I owned and being estranged from my kids has caused me to be anxious about money. My new wife is rich and can support me, but I am an old-fashioned guy and I'm torn up inside over this." It was clear to Marcee that they needed an estate plan that would consider these feelings, and that taxes had no bearing on these feelings. She said to him, "Your wife has money from her inherited trust. You have money from your business, which is a sole proprietorship. Since this asset is now community property, let's have Joan (who agreed) sign the entire business over to you so you can leave it to anyone you want in your will. You will know that what is yours will remain yours and what is Joan's will be hers. You have both agreed that you would want the house (which was owned solely by Joan) to be owned jointly." The essence of this plan is that both Joan and Dick are happy and feel in control. Her assets will go to her children, and his estate to his kids. She uses her money for their support, and Dick's money is used for "fun" things.

This was a successful plan because Marcee stuck with it until she got it right, and had the competence and creativity to offer the solution to a problem that many estate planners would have never uncovered. We cannot emphasize enough the importance of good discovery and dialogue before offering recommendations to your clients. Imagine how this would have turned out if Marcee had clouded the process with a discussion of the estate tax laws.

END-OF-LIFE QUESTIONS

We all know the adage about not getting a second chance to make a first impression, but we do get an opportunity to alter people's opinions of us later. One thing is certain, however. When leaving a legacy, you never get a second chance to make a last impression!

The Mayo Clinic lists "The Three Big End-of-Life Questions":

1. What was the meaning of my life?
2. Did I make a difference in the world?
3. What is my legacy to the world?

When clients are approached properly and asked the right questions, it is our experience that they are more concerned about how they will be remembered than how much tax planning they did before they died. It is our job, as financial life planners, to remind our clients and make sure that their estate plan and the legacy they leave reflect their core values.

CHAPTER 8 SUMMARY

- An important question to ask clients is, "How do you want to be remembered?"
- Avoid having tax savings drive estate planning decisions.
- Probe inconsistencies and reconcile them before making recommendations.
- Clients' estate plans need to reflect their core values.
- When leaving a legacy, you never get a second chance to make a last impression.

9 Philanthropy— The Power of Giving

We make a living by what we get. We make a life by what we give.

—Winston Churchill

GPA

I recently attended an event hosted by my alma mater (Temple University) at the Philadelphia Art Museum. It was a Dali exhibit, funded by Dennis Alter, a Temple alumnus and president of Advanta Corporation. He has done a great deal for Temple and the community, and he spoke that evening about how undergraduates are consumed with their GPA (grade point average). Now that we have graduated, he told us, we should also be concerned with our GPA, which he defined as a *Grand Purpose Activity*. All of us, he said, owe it to the community to give back something that for us would be our GPA. I thought about that and my own personal giving. But I also considered how helping my clients to discover their GPAs would be a way to multiply my efforts. We have a great responsibility to help our clients reach their goals. Often, those goals include philanthropy, but they may not know how giving more will affect their futures. It is our job to show them.

THE CHARITABLE GIVING BUG

When Nicole first came to see us, she was 62 and had just retired from a career of teaching. Most of her investment portfolio of about $2 million consisted of assets in a 403(b) plan and several annuities that her previous financial adviser had sold her. As a result, just about everything she owned was in tax-deferred accounts. She was single and had no children, but she had several nieces and nephews to whom she wanted to leave her estate when she died. At the time, the maximum estate tax exemption amount was $650,000. While tax implications should not drive estate planning decisions, it is our duty to help our clients by recommending the most tax-efficient methods of accomplishing their goals. Her problem was that almost all of her assets would be subject to both income and estate taxes when she died.

When we inquired about her charitable giving objectives, she told us that she always wanted to do more but she "never got around to it." We asked her if she would be open to a strategy that would provide for charitable bequests at her death, but would not affect the money she wanted to leave her nieces and nephews. She wanted to know more, so we described how a charitable remainder trust might work if she named the trust beneficiary of some of her annuities. We told her that she could name several charities or just one. She seemed interested, so we ran the numbers for her. Our projections (assuming she died in 20 years) showed that the present value of the income her heirs would have received from the trust would have been $3,093,000—only slightly less than the $3,143,000 under her present plan. However, 20 years after her death, the charities would receive $3,773,000. These numbers were very compelling and she agreed to have her attorney prepare the documents. At one of our meetings, she asked for suggestions for charitable beneficiaries. We told her to be observant and think about causes or organizations that she had an interest in helping, and she eventually settled on three organizations, which were named in the trust. What ensued was remarkable.

Several months later, she asked us if she could begin to donate money to those charities now, and began doing so. About a year after that, she decided to change the beneficiaries on several of the annuities so that the charities would receive some money outright at her death rather than waiting for 20 years after her death. A little over a year later, she changed her entire estate plan and left smaller specific bequests to her nieces and nephews with the balance of her assets, including her IRA, going to endowments for the benefit of the charities. What happened to cause this change in her thinking? I believe that she caught the "giving bug." She also came to the realization that she was providing money for her relatives not because they needed it but because she felt obligated to do so. How many of our clients would do something similar if presented with the choice and the opportunity?

PEOPLE WHO GIVE ARE HAPPIER AND HEALTHIER

While it seems intuitively true that people who are generous with their resources benefit from that generosity, there's evidence to suggest that it's factually true, as well. According to the Institute of HeartMath, "People who give money to charity often experience joy and satisfaction in having given. By deciding to make a difference in someone else's life, they give more meaning to their own." In *Psychology Today*, heart specialist Dr. Herbert Benson states, "For millennia, people have been describing techniques on how to forget oneself, how to experience decreased metabolic rates, lower blood pressure, lower heart rates and other health benefits. Altruism works this way, just as do yoga, spirituality, and meditation." In addition, George Vaillant, in his book *Adaptation to Life*, concluded that adopting an altruistic lifestyle is a critical component of mental health.

Therefore, it is very important that we ask our clients about their core values, and point out any differences between those values and their plans. If philanthropy is a core value and leaving assets to their children is described as an obligation (an "ought to" in our questionnaire), that needs to be pursued. Psychologists who study happiness and what makes people happy tell us that money, position, power, and even health, are not the things that distinguish happy people from unhappy people. As stated above, people who give tend to be happier and healthier, and we point that out to our clients. As John Templeton has written, "Happiness comes from spiritual wealth, not material wealth... Happiness comes from giving, not getting. If we try hard to bring happiness to others, we cannot stop it from coming to us also. To get joy, we must give it, and to keep joy, we must scatter it."

THE POWER OF ENDOWMENTS

I serve on Temple University's Planned Giving Advisory Board, and University President David Adamany addressed our board one day and shared his story with us. In the mid-1950s, Harvard was primarily a university that drew its students from the northeast, and they wanted to find qualified candidates from other regions. Mr. Adamany, who was from Wisconsin, was offered a full scholarship and he accepted. His mother told him to be sure to find out who provided the endowment that funded his scholarship so he could write a letter of gratitude. The administrator at Harvard informed him that he would be unable to write that letter because the last living member of the family who funded the endowment had died 100 years earlier! We share this story with our clients who show an interest in charitable giving because it demonstrates the power of providing endowments, which have the ability to give in perpetuity.

ENCOURAGING CLIENTS TO GIVE

Harv Ames, CFP®, who practices in New Hampshire, encourages charitable giving among his clients with a matching gift program. "In the past we used to look at tax returns to discover people's charitable tendencies," says Harv, "but we discovered that tax returns alone don't tell the whole story. Since implementing this program, we have discovered that clients have been contributing more than they did previously." The following is a letter he sends to his clients each year:

> It is that time of year when our thoughts turn toward a season of giving thanks and of sharing. As in the past, we would like to help you with any charitable giving that you

may contemplate for this year. We believe that, overall, our "client family" is thankful for the blessings of good health, good family, and good friends. We are also thankful for our ability to share with those we love and care about, as well as for the community or world at large. Perhaps, in some small way, we can share with others less fortunate or with organizations providing services that are helped by our donations.

Thus, Ames Planning Associates is pleased to announce our annual Charitable Gift Matching Program for clients whereby we will match the amount of your charitable contribution, on a dollar-for-dollar basis, up to a maximum total of $50 to the legally recognized charity(ies) of your choice. Thus, this allows us to augment and expand your gifting program to your favorite charity.

If this appeals to you, please take a moment to write the name of your favorite charity on the enclosed form. Please write your charity's address on a business-size envelope and enclose your check payable to that charity. Send all three items to us no later than December 2nd, so we can contribute to your chosen charity this calendar year. We will mail your donation, along with our matching contribution, directly to your charity.

Our best wishes to you for a thoughtful season of giving.

Ross Levin and all of his partners are members of the "1 Percent Club," where all members commit to giving 5 percent of their income or 1 percent of their net worth each year. They share this with their clients, many of whom increase their own giving as a result.

Rich and Gayle Colman make sure that time is allotted to have a specific conversation about philanthropy with each of their clients. "This is often done as we move through the initial stages of the planning process and we become clearer about what the long-term asset base is reasonably anticipated to be," says Rich. "We also ask them what societal issues are important and of interest to them, and conduct the conversation from the perspective of 'needs' and how might their legacy touch the lives of entities or people who are committed to that cause."

While we do not attempt to instill our values about giving, we feel that we need to go beyond the superficial discovery of looking at a tax return to determine if clients desire to give. We have given examples in earlier chapters of clients who previously had given very little but wanted to do more. Such was the situation for Ben and Joan. During our discovery process, he told us of his desire to contribute a large amount of money to his alma mater, if not during his lifetime, via a request in his will. Joan, however, was reluctant and concerned for her own future and her grandchildren. Initially, we were told to proceed with our planning without the bequest. Since bringing their estate plan up to date was a high priority for them, we held a meeting devoted to that issue. Once again, I asked each of them the following question: "Ideally, what would you want to happen at your death?" Joan told us that she was most concerned about outliving their money and that she wanted anything that was left to go to her children and grandchildren. Ben, however, restated his desire to donate a substantial sum to the university. This time, however, he began to well up as he told us how important this was to him. I felt that we could no longer ignore this goal, so I asked Joan if she had observed Ben's face when he told us about his goal. She said she did, but she felt that the university did not need the money and she might. Would she be willing, I asked, to consider Ben's desire if it did not affect her lifestyle? They had a very good marriage of over 50 years, and, knowing how important this had become for Ben, she was willing to listen. Ironically, while she was aware of Ben's goal, she told us, "I never knew how important it was to him until today."

We showed them how a charitable remainder trust would work and that it would pay income while either one was alive. Of course, the children and grandchildren would inherit less, but they were willing to accept that since our projections estimated that there would be sufficient assets for them. They decided to transfer $500,000 in the trust. She was assured the income and he was able to fulfill a life-long dream. It will probably come as no surprise for you to know that I believe that one of our jobs, as financial life planners, is to encourage philanthropy. We have the ability to make a huge difference in our communities by showing our clients how they can find their "GPA." We don't expect people to adopt our values about giving, but we also don't accept a tax return as the only evidence that people are charitably inclined. Ben and Joan's returns certainly provided us with no clues. It is through thorough discovery that we uncover these desires. I suppose we could have concluded that Ben's goals could not be fulfilled because Joan objected. Instead, we felt that it was our obligation to find a way to make it work.

Dave Ramsey has written,

> Personal growth requires that you give money away. The institutions to which you give will survive if you don't give, but you will have missed an opportunity to benefit.

Somehow giving reminds us that the world does not revolve around us and that no matter what our financial status is, someone always is in a much worse situation. Good things that cannot be calculated or quantified are set in motion in your life and in your finances when you give.

We want to do our part to help our clients experience the joys of giving.

DISCOVERING CLIENTS' CHARITABLE GIVING GOALS

There are several places in the discovery process that will help you to uncover how important philanthropy is to your clients. In the first questionnaire they are given to complete, the Financial Life Checkup, one of the areas they are asked to rate is "… my level of charitable giving." One of the major categories in the Life Transitions questionnaire is "charitable/legacy." In the Defining True Wealth questionnaire, they are asked to complete the statement, "I want to be remembered someday as…" In the Dreams, Visions, and Images for Use of Wealth questionnaire, we discover whether they consider charitable giving as a "heart's core" value. One of the interview questions we ask each client is, "What part does philanthropy play in your value system?" Often giving more to charity shows up in one or more of the three Kinder scenarios. When they are asked to list their life goals, one of the categories is "charitable." And, finally, we learn a great deal from the Benevolence Survey.

It is our experience that one of the reasons for the disconnect between clients' charitable giving values and their actions is that they do not believe they have the resources to give. Others may feel an obligation to leave all assets to their children. Often, the long-term projections will estimate that they will die with much more money than they dreamed possible, and this knowledge may cause them to adopt a planned giving program. Whatever it may be, it is our job to show them what is possible. We have seen major positive transformations, some of which we have described in this and other chapters, when clients are shown how to align their values with their money. When I think about how much good we can do for our clients and others, I am convinced that *there is no calling greater than financial life planning.*

CHAPTER 9 SUMMARY
- We all need to discover our Grand Purpose Activity (GPA).
- People who catch the "giving bug" will usually be happier as a result.
- Providing funds for endowments can be very motivating and rewarding because they can live long beyond our own lives.
- Consider adopting programs and systems that encourage your clients to give.
- We need to look beyond tax returns to discover our clients' charitable giving values.

10 | *Marketing: Meet Ralph Busco*

Marketing is…the whole business seen…
from the customer's point of view.

—Peter Drucker

"This may be one of the most stressful years of your life." That is what many of our friends told us when we informed them that we had purchased a lot and were going to have a home built. Builders, they warned us, were notorious for delays, hidden charges, shoddy workmanship, nonresponsiveness, and other ills. Soon, they assured us, we would be either reconsidering our decision to build or visiting a therapist to get an understanding of the underlying cause of our propensity for self-punishment.

They were wrong! Please meet Ralph Busco, World-Class Builder. To understand the success of this builder, there are two things you need to know. First, unbelievably, his number is unlisted because

100 percent of his business comes from referrals from satisfied customers, which brings us the second item. Each year, he rents a country club in the area and invites everyone he has ever built a home for to a gala dinner. Most builders would not dare do that for fear of lynching. These affairs, however, are "love-fests" for Ralph. I have never met anyone who ever said anything negative about Ralph or his or her home-building experience. That is certainly an enviable position for anyone who owns a business or wants to attract new business. So, what is it that makes Ralph so special, and what can we learn from him and his successful marketing plan?

BUILDING A HOME—AN ENJOYABLE EXPERIENCE

Our favorable experience began when we were choosing a builder and interviewed Ralph. Of course, we were pre-sold by the people who referred him, but we still thought it prudent to screen several builders before making a selection. We noticed a difference almost immediately. When we asked the other builders what we would need to do next if we decided to go ahead, they spoke of contracts, deposits, etc. Ralph said a handshake would be appropriate. The other builders told us that they would begin their process after the architect's plans were completed. Ralph told us that he would like to be at every meeting with our architect. "Wouldn't that require a contract and a deposit?" we asked. "Not necessary," he said. "We do have a handshake, after all." In any event, he told us that there was no way he could price the project until we finalized our plans, but he assured us that he would point out features that would put us over budget. That was why he wanted to accompany us to the meetings with our architect.

When the plans were completed, he visited us with an

agreement. The cost of the entire project was itemized and he disclosed to us what his profit would be, as well as which work he was marking up and which he was not. The bottom line for him, he said, was set. He instructed his contractors and vendors to pass their cost for any upgrades directly to us with no further markups. His profit was fair, he told us, and he saw no need to make more on the project. For example, he did not think it was appropriate for builders to make money on the cost of appliances, tile, countertops, etc. He would recommend vendors to us and instruct them to pass any builder cost savings to us. For advisers who have told me that they neither want nor need to disclose all of their compensation, I would like to have them talk to me about the power of full disclosure. They need to meet Ralph Busco.

When we signed the agreement, we began to write a check as stated in the contract. "What are you doing?" he asked. "I won't need any of your money until I need to pay my subcontractors." This was months and many meetings with the architect since that original handshake, and no money had yet been paid. He said he believed that he had no right to hold our money before he needed to begin the project.

I could recount the process of watching our home develop into what we dreamed it could be, but I can say that the journey was delightful. How many people do you know who have had homes built who would use that word to describe their experience? The story, of course, does not end here. He personally saw to it that any items that required tweaking after we took possession were promptly taken care of. The people who referred us were having problems with their maple floors expanding and contracting.

He tried to solve the problem, but could not. In spite of the fact that he had cautioned them about using maple, three years after the home was completed he refunded the cost of the floor!

RALPH BUSCO'S MARKETING STRATEGY

When our home was done, we decided to take Ralph and his wife to dinner as a way of thanking him for the splendid job he did. He knew the owner of the restaurant but had not seen him for several years, and they reminisced about the "old days." It became apparent to me that they once were blackjack dealers at one of the casinos in Atlantic City. How, I wondered, do you go from dealer to world-class builder? Later that week, I called Ralph to find out. His story is a marketing lesson for all of us. Several years ago, he told us, his parents hired a builder to do major renovations on their home. They asked Ralph to help with the negotiations, follow-up, etc. The experience was horrendous. The builder would promise to be there on a certain day and would neither come nor call. When Ralph would call and leave messages, his calls were not returned. The project was completed months after the promised date at a cost of thousands more than estimated. Moreover, much of the work was not done properly and it took almost a year for him to correct it. Ralph could not understand how someone could stay in business with such poor service. He discovered, after relating his story to his friends, that this builder was not atypical. Ralph's conclusion after this experience was that "the world needed a better builder," and he decided that he could be the one, in spite of the fact that he had no home-building experience.

Ralph interviewed people who had recently built homes and asked them four questions:

1. What did your builder do that you wish he had not?
2. What didn't your builder do that you wish he had?
3. What did you like best about the experience?
4. What did you like least?

The answers to these questions led to the development of his marketing plan. Some of the things they said they did not like, for instance, were the cost overruns, marking up appliances, subcontractors who did not show up when promised, failure to return phone calls, lack of follow-up after the job, and seeming more interested in new business than in serving existing customers. His plan was to do all of the things customers wanted their builders to do and not do any of the things that they did not want them to do. This seems simple enough, but not many businesses devise their marketing strategies around such a basic tenet: *"Give them what they want!"* If they did, there would not be the cry we hear so often today: "Whatever happened to customer service?"

Ralph did one other thing. He asked people who the best subcontractors were because he knew his success would be predicated not only on excellent service, but also on quality construction. He approached these contractors and asked one question: "What do I need to do to have you make me your number one priority?" Of course, remaining consistent in his thinking, Ralph did what they asked, such as paying them promptly, and he soon became their favorite builder. While our home was being built, we often wondered why subcontractors would leave other projects they were working on for other builders to correct something at our house. We later discovered that this was a part of Ralph's strategy and marketing plan.

"BUILDING" A MARKETING PLAN

There are wonderful lessons that we can learn from Ralph Busco. Many years ago, a marketing consultant told us that we were among the best marketers he had ever encountered. We were surprised by this remark because we did not devote much time to overt marketing, so we asked him what he meant. "You deliver more service than your clients expect and that leads to client retention, referrals, and the growth of your business," he replied. "If that isn't marketing, I do not know what is." Ralph understands that, and he has built one of the most successful building companies in the area. You can follow his lead. Make a list of what you believe clients want their financial planners to do that most do not. Then make another list of what financial planners do that clients do not want them to do. You may also want to survey clients and non-clients with the same questions. You can build a very strong marketing plan by listening to what they have to say. Most people think of marketing as doing something overt such as advertising or conducting seminars, but what is more powerful than providing top-notch, unusual service?

Listed below are some of the things we have implemented in our practice over the years to set ourselves apart from other advisers. Some of these practices and procedures were initiated based on the things that bother me about doing business with other service companies, and others by inter-viewing and surveying our clients. We also ask prospects why they have chosen to change advisers. The initial response may be, "My portfolio isn't performing." However, with more probing, we usually discover that the problems are in areas over which the adviser has significantly more control than market fluctuations. As you can see, the list below is not technical, and we know competence is vital to keeping and attracting clients. However, many advisers with professional expertise do not attract or keep enough clients to have a profitable and viable business.

OUR FIRM'S "RALPH BUSCO" LIST

- *Calls are always answered by a live person during regular business hours.* If I dislike not being able to talk to a person when I need to, I can only assume that I am not alone. Our clients have confirmed this when we've asked. As Theo Michelson of State Farm has said, "People don't want to communicate with an organization or a computer. They want to talk to a real, live, responsive, responsible person who will listen and help them get satisfaction."
- *Callers are never automatically placed in voice mail.* How many times have we returned a person's call only to be transferred to voice mail without an opportunity to tell the receptionist that you are merely returning his call? This is particularly disturbing when the person whose call you are returning is trying to sell you something. We, of course, have voice mail, but callers are not transferred to it unless they request it. In most cases, a friendly receptionist takes the message. Often, someone else in the office may be available to help.
- *Clients, prospects, and others are never addressed by their first names unless we are invited to do so.* I can never understand someone hiring an 18-year-old receptionist, not training her properly, and having her address a 60-year-old client as "Bob." I know that this will not offend everyone, but I am sure that it will upset some people, because it upsets me.

So why take the chance of doing that if we know that calling people by their last names will offend no one?

- *All calls received by clients before 3 p.m. are returned that day.* Calls received after 3 p.m. are returned by 10 a.m. the next day. Many prospects have told us that the reason they are firing their current advisers is that they are not responsive and do not return calls. We know that it may not be feasible for the planner servicing the account to return some calls the same day, but we are careful to warn clients of that in advance, and, if necessary, someone else handles the issue.
- *All service requests received before 3 p.m. are handled the same business day*
- *Client calls are returned first.* It may be tempting to return a call from that prospect you have been trying to convert, but our number one priority is our clients.
- *Clients and prospects are never to be kept waiting for more than ten minutes.* When I have an appointment with a doctor or other professional and I am not seen until 30 or more minutes after the scheduled time of my appointment, I feel that she is telling me that her time is more valuable than mine. We never want to give our clients that impression, so we schedule times between appointments far enough apart that we know we can see them promptly.
- *Coffee and tea are served in real china, not Styrofoam cups.* You would not serve your guests in inferior cups, so why do so with your clients? This is a part of making the experience special. More about that later.
- *No one in our office ever says, "That is not my job."* If the person answering the phone has no knowledge of the client's need, he is trained to help by transferring the call

to someone who has the knowledge. Our clients need to know that everyone in our firm is willing to help. They feel special every time they call.

- *Resolve errors immediately after they are discovered and, when correcting, always err on the side of the client.* All companies and people make mistakes. What separates the fair from the outstanding is the way they are corrected. We do so much to correct the miscue that the client often comes out better off than he was before the mistake was made. In a *Wall Street Journal* review of the book *Satisfaction* (Chris Denove and James D. Power IV, Portfolio), Paul Carroll writes, "The authors also offer up the occasional surprise. Customers who run into problems but whose problems are handled swiftly and politely actually wind up being more loyal than customers who never encounter a problem in the first place." That is no surprise to us. We have had clients mention the way we handled a situation many years after the incident. Referrals from clients have mentioned this to us when at their initial visit. Remember how Ralph Busco handled the maple floors? Those clients will tell everyone they know that story.

- *Remember that every client or prospect is a potential spokesperson for your firm and they will share both good and bad experiences.*

- *We place fresh flowers in the reception area and conference room and change them weekly.*

- *If you have the ability to do it—do it!* It is our job as financial planners to help make our clients' financial lives easier and stress-free. For example, if a client wants to "park" some money he may need for liquidity, we may recommend a high-interest money market account. However, we will go beyond giving him an 800 number to call. We will complete and mail the application for him.

- *Deliver more than you promise and more than other advisers.* Exceeding clients' expectations is a sure way to retain them and have them refer others to you. The authors of *Satisfaction* write, "One sure way to send your customer satisfaction plummeting is to overpromise and under-deliver." As a matter of fact, they tell us that exceeding expectations is more important than high performance.

- *Make the experience memorable.* Our goal is to have every client who visits our office remark that the experience was enjoyable and special. We accomplish that goal by doing some of the items that I listed above (coffee service, warm greetings, etc.), but it goes beyond that. If our aim is to reduce or eliminate money worries for our clients, our meetings focus on whatever is necessary to achieve that. Throughout this book, we have stressed the need to understand our clients' goals and aspirations. When concerns such as a falling market hinder their opportunity to live free of stress, we always remind them of the effect the issue may have on their goals—not their money. It may be easy to tell them that the market will recover because it always has, but we have found that may do little to allay their current fears. In any event, they do not need to hear the obvious—what almost all other advisers will tell them. We discuss the effect the market correction will have on their ability to achieve their goals, even if it does not fully recover. Our goal as financial life planners is not to justify our investment strategy. It is to have them leave our office feeling better than when they arrived. Almost all of our clients tell us that they do.

Ralph Busco certainly is not alone in his approach to giving people what they want. Successful businesses, large and small, prosper when they do. In *Satisfaction*, the authors tell of a small plumber who promised his customers two things: all of his employees would wear clean shirts and they would show up on time. (He knew that people complained about workers who came into their homes smelling bad and those who did not come when promised.) These two little changes set him apart from his competitors and he grew into one of the largest and most successful plumbing companies in the area. Many financial planners believe that being competent and dispensing good advice is all that is necessary to build their businesses, but marketing requires that they set themselves apart from other advisers who are just as competent. Providing the financial life planning services outlined in this book will help you to do that. You may also want to follow Ralph Busco's example by "giving them what they want." Build your own list of qualities, as Ralph has, and implement them in your practice, as we have. Your list may be quite different, but if it works for a builder, there is no reason it will not work for all of us. Ralph would be very delighted to know that he has helped not only those who build houses, but financial advisers who build businesses.

CHAPTER 10 SUMMARY

- The key to marketing is to "Give them what they want."
- Survey your clients and others to determine what they like and dislike about financial advisers and build a marketing strategy around the results.
- Make the experience memorable for your clients.
- Always exceed expectations.

- Resolve all problems promptly and err on the side of the client when doing so.
- The little things you do matter. For example, clients will remember that they were served coffee and tea in china cups, that fresh flowers were placed in your office, and that calls are returned promptly.

11 | *Ongoing Service: The Key to Client Retention*

> *Begin with the end in mind.*
>
> —Stephen Covey

When we purchased our first boat, other boaters advised us that we would experience two things for sure. First, the boat would need maintenance to correct problems—both major and minor. The adage we heard most often was, "After all, it is a boat." Second, we would find it very difficult to have someone service it in a timely fashion, so we should expect downtime when we would rather be enjoying the water. The first was true, but, fortunately, our boat dealer had an excellent and very responsive service department. Often, we would call first thing in the morning and the problem (if it was minor) would be corrected that same morning, in time for us to use the boat. We called the owner of the dealership to compliment him on the courtesy, competence, and responsiveness of Carl, his service manager. He thanked us and said, "Our sales people sell the first boat our customers buy from us. Carl sells all others."

THE IMPORTANCE OF CLIENT RETENTION

It puzzles me that many financial advisers place more emphasis on obtaining new clients than they do on retaining existing ones. The answer to the following question may be a gauge for who you value most. You return from lunch and have two messages. One is from a client you have had for five years and the other from a prospect you have been trying to convert to a client. What call do you return first? The decision we make at our firm is based on one irrefutable fact. The pain we suffer when a client is lost cannot be made up by the joy we may experience when we establish a relationship with a new client. That is why clients' calls are the first we return.

The paradox is that keeping clients will invariably result in more new clients for two obvious reasons. First, it will increase your referral base. Ex-clients don't refer people to you. In addition, high retention will be evidence that your clients are pleased with your service and therefore more likely to refer new clients to your firm. How many of us have considered the measurable value of keeping clients? The following illustrates this value for two hypothetical firms and is based on the following assumptions:

- The average annual revenue per client in the first year illustrated is $5,000, and increases at the rate of 5 percent per year.
- Each firm has 100 clients and gross revenue of $500,000 in the first year.
- Each firm brings in 12 new clients each year at an average

annual fee of $5,000 (also increasing at the rate of 5 percent per year).

- Firm A retains 85 percent of its clients each year; Firm B retains 95 percent.
- By the end of the ten-year period illustrated, the average fee per client has increased to $8,150 for each firm.

The following are the gross revenue results for each firm:

Year	Firm A	Firm B
5	$ 567,945	$ 899,799
10	$684,600	$1,328,450

During the ten-year period illustrated, Firm A has increased its revenue by 3.19 percent per year and Firm B by 10.26 percent. If similar increases were to occur over another ten years, Firm A would gross about $777,000, while Firm B's gross would be over $3,500,000!

None of the above takes into consideration the highly likely scenario that Firm B will be attracting many more clients because its referral base of clients has increased from 100 to 163 in the ten-year period while Firm A's has actually fallen to 84! I suggest that you do a similar exercise for your firm, if you have not already done so. Client retention—not marketing—is the key to growth. And that being the case, we need to provide service to make us almost indispensable to our clients.

ONGOING SERVICE—THINK WITH THE END IN MIND
When prospective clients ask us about continuing service, we jokingly tell them that we will do anything they need, but "we will not cut your lawn!" In reality, we want them to look to us to help them through all of their financial issues.

In fact, the way we are paid (see Chapter 14) encourages them to call us because our fee includes all services. Earlier, we discussed the differences between money managers and financial life planners. To paraphrase Stephen Covey, to provide quality service, we must think with the end in mind. The "end" for money managers is portfolio performance. For financial life planners it is much broader than that. While helping our clients with their investments is important, we need to assure them that it is always done in the context of reaching their unique goals. If we limit our continuing service to managing their assets, we are not fulfilling the purpose of our firm, which is to provide financial peace of mind for our clients. Actually, our firm's stated purpose is "To improve the quality of our clients' lives." Of course, that includes many areas that are not investment-related. To list all of the services we have provided for clients over the years would be impractical. However, it is important to note that we will do whatever they need, always mindful of the end. Providing service is not the goal—helping our clients improve the quality of their lives by facilitating financial peace of mind is the goal, and we do not limit what we will do to achieve it. My boat dealer's goal was not to provide prompt service. That was merely a tactic to achieve his more important goal—satisfied clients who would purchase their next boat from them. It is a subtle difference, but an enormous one when one is developing plans for serving existing clients.

Most people have experienced the frustration of taking a car in for service for a problem, getting the car back and discovering the problem still exists. We complain to the service manager who tells us that he replaced a part because it was defective. Perhaps he did, but that is not why we brought the car in for service. Yet, he saw that as a perfectly legitimate response to the complaint! He defined his job as providing a service (replacing a defective part). The response would have been much different if his "end" was solving a problem. Some financial advisers judge their ongoing service by how much they do. Clients, however judge us on the results we achieve. And I do not necessarily mean investment performance. If our end goal for clients is to help them achieve financial peace of mind, we need to do whatever we believe is necessary to get to that end. Unhappy clients will not be consoled by proclamations that we devoted lots of time to their accounts. The fact that they know we are available to help them sort out issues and make intelligent financial decisions is important to provide that peace of mind.

NUMBER OF MEETINGS

I once attended a session at an FPA meeting and the presenting planner was discussing a client with whom she felt she was having a problem. It was her policy to have quarterly meetings, and this particular client did not want to meet with her this often. She was asking the audience for advice on how they handle similar situations. One of the planners in attendance asked her some very cogent questions:

• How long had he been a client? Six years, she answered.
• Has he complained about the service? No, she replied.
• Do you stay in touch with him to discuss important issues by telephone? Yes.
• Does he ever call you when he needs advice? Yes, occasionally he does.

- So what is the problem? She had no answer for this question, the most important one he asked.

Rather than make decisions about when we will meet with our clients, we leave it up to them once the initial planning process is complete. We do think it is important to have face-to-face meetings (at least annually), but it is a rare client that finds it necessary to meet as often as quarterly. Since our retention is about 98 percent, it seems to fit them just fine. In fact, we are confident that we would lose some clients who don't feel a need to meet quarterly if we insisted that they do so. Here is a unique concept—give them what *they* want—not what *you* think is necessary. Some planners have frequent meetings, it seems, to justify the fees their clients pay them. Our clients understand that their fees are retainers for all of the services they may require. A planner once told me that clients do not pay us to be there all of the time. They pay us to be there when they need us. In addition, if we are spending too much time in quarterly meetings that are unnecessary to our clients and us, there is the possibility that we will not have the time to provide timely service when our clients really need it. Remember to think with the end in mind. What is the end for your clients? We believe it should be to help your clients reach their goals and live their lives free of anxiety about money. Clients do not measure their success by the number of meetings they attend, and neither do we.

SERVICES PROVIDED

As discussed above, we provide a wide range of services for our clients, because we want them to know that we are there for them when they need us. While it would be virtually impossible to list all of the issues that come before us, I have chosen to list a sampling of some of the services we do provide for our clients. Of course, it is not meant to be a complete list, and I have not listed the most obvious, such as constructing investment policies, selecting appropriate investments, portfolio rebalancing, cash flow management, etc. It is most important to remember that you need to *create a service culture in your firm that everyone, from planners to part-time clerical employees, understands and in which they participate.*

- **Income Tax Management.** While our firm has chosen not to provide tax preparation, we do believe that reducing our clients' tax burdens (and increasing their after-tax returns) is a core service that our clients appreciate. Of course, we provide tax advice to our clients during the initial planning process. This chapter, however, is about follow-up service and how to help clients on a continuing basis. When we manage our clients' assets, we find that there are a number of things (beyond the obvious recommendations such as buying tax-free bonds, tax-efficient mutual funds, placing the high-tax assets in qualified accounts where possible, etc.) that can significantly reduce the taxes they pay. Some of these tactics would be difficult for most clients to implement on their own. As a result, we increase our value-added and their financial peace of mind. The following tax strategies are implemented for all of our clients for whom we manage taxable assets:
  - *Don't pay taxes on gains that you don't have.* We all know that one of the disadvantages of owning mutual funds (our primary investment vehicle) is that capital gains are distributed regardless of the gain (or loss) experienced by the owner of that fund. For example, assume that your

client had invested $50,000 in a fund and at the end of the year the value is still $50,000. However, the fund company is declaring a capital gain distribution of $5,000. That client would be responsible for paying tax on money she had not made. We assure our clients that we will see to it that they never pay taxes on gains they do not have. In some cases, our clients may have actually lost money and, despite that, if nothing is done they will need to pay income taxes on an investment that has a net loss! In order to avoid that, our firm produces a spreadsheet in December of each year that lists each client's unrealized gains or losses in each fund they own. This is compared to the gain they would experience if they held the fund and accepted the distribution. With some exceptions for small differences, the fund is sold before the distribution if its effect is a better tax result for the client. As with all tax harvesting (see below), a similar fund is purchased (being careful to do so after the distribution date for the new fund) so the client is not out of the market.

– *Whenever possible, rebalance with money on which you have already paid taxes.* Reinvesting dividends and capital gains may be appropriate if you never intend to rebalance your clients' portfolios, but doing so will cause unnecessary taxes for them if you believe that rebalancing is a strategy you plan to implement. Let's assume that you are reinvesting all distributions and you find that a mutual fund that your client owns with a position of $50,000 (a cost basis of $25,000) needs to be reduced to $40,000, so you sell $10,000 and pay a capital gains tax on $5,000 (the cost basis is 50 percent of the value, assuming you use an average cost). The federal tax will be $750 (15 percent). We will also assume that distributions from the fund during the previous year (which were reinvested) equaled $5,000. If you took that distribution in cash, your fund would now be worth $45,000 (assuming no gain or loss) and the cost basis $20,000 (reduced by the $5,000 distribution since it was not reinvested) or 44.44 percent of the fund's value (decreased from 50 percent if reinvested). In order to rebalance the portfolio, we would only need to sell $5,000 to reduce the holding to $40,000, so your client would pay a capital gains tax on $2,778 (55.56 percent of the sale), and a federal tax of $416.70. When we apply this strategy across the entire portfolio, it can result in significant tax savings for your clients. Of course, the downside is that it will result in higher transaction fees, but we have found that the tax savings more than compensate for these expenses.

– *Volatility can be your friend.* It has always puzzled me that so many financial planners wait until year-end to do tax harvesting. Of course, markets can be volatile throughout the year, so tax harvesting needs to be done when we have the opportunity. Recoveries can be rapid, and if we wait until the end of the year, we may discover that the losses we could have taken earlier are no longer available. Of course, if you wait 30 days to get back in, your clients may not experience the gains of a quick recovery, so it is extremely important that the money from the investments you sell for tax purposes is reinvested in similar investments.

• **Periodic Updates.** When I first began practicing financial planning in 1983, our firm would provide its clients with a detailed financial *plan*. It contained recommendations for insurance, investments, taxes, estate planning, etc. We would implement the approved recommendations and periodically review the investment portfolios. If I were to honestly judge what we did in those days, I would not call it financial plan*ning*. We sold financial plans and the products to implement those plans. However, at some point, we realized that what we do is called financial planning, and that title assumes an ongoing, dynamic process. Therefore, we periodically update all of our planning. We run new scenarios based on changing circumstances. We re-run the numbers even if their situation has not changed. We always keep the end in mind—improving the quality of our clients' lives by providing financial peace of mind for our clients. Demonstrating that they are still on target to reach their goals or need to make changes to get back on track helps them to stay focused on living free of worries about money. A client called us in 2002 (near the end of the bear market), to express concern that her portfolio was close to falling below an arbitrary amount that she felt was necessary for her to reach her goals. This was a conclusion that she came to on her own, which had very little to do with her ability to reach her goals. Nevertheless, she was concerned and it was affecting her ability to live free from money worries. In order to allay her fears and get her back on track to the peace of mind that was eluding her, we ran various scenarios for her—each with considerably less than she assumed she needed. All demonstrated that she had no reason to fear and she left our office feeling much better about her situation. Had we made the conversation about the market and the need to stay the course, we are doubtful that the outcome would have been as positive for her. Our clients hear negativity from so-called pundits, and we need to remind them of why they invest in the first place—to reach their goals! They also need to *keep the end in mind.*

- **Quarterbacking the Team.** As financial life planners, we consider ourselves the quarterbacks of our clients' teams of advisers, which may include their accountants, lawyers, and insurance agents. While these other advisers may be quite competent, they each will (and should) concentrate on their areas of expertise. Our experience has taught us that it is a rare adviser who knows as much about our clients as we do. We need to be assured that all recommendations will be compatible with all of our clients' goals and needs. And we need to *keep the end in mind.*

Because some of these professionals may have a myopic view of their situations, our clients have found it very helpful for us to be an integral part of the dialogue to add a more holistic perspective.

For example, Ernie and Joanne were both in their second marriages and each had children. He owned a homebuilding business and his son was in the business with him. Aside from the money he had tied up in land and building projects, he had very few liquid assets. He wanted to start a new development, but he had exhausted his line of credit and his bank would not grant additional funds until some of his current projects were complete. Joanne, on the other hand, owned several properties free and clear of debt as well as liquid assets. Whenever he needed additional advances from the bank for new projects, Joanne pledged her assets as collateral. Based on the provisions of their prenuptial agreement, she would inherit half of the business and its assets at his death. Ernie wanted to be assured that his son, Al, would get the entire business when he died, and Joanne felt that this was unfair since her assets were being used as collateral for many of the projects. She called me to inform me that she had retained the services of a real estate attorney to "see that I get all that I should if Ernie were to die." They had scheduled a meeting at the lawyer's office and I asked if I could attend, since I was very familiar with their financial situation as well as their goals. She and Ernie agreed that it would be a good idea.

The lawyer opened the conversation by making it clear that he was representing Joanne, and that she was entitled to her share of the business because her assets were at risk. Leaving the business to Ernie's son would have deprived her of her legitimate claim, he said. As he presented his case, I felt as if I were in a divorce settlement meeting and an adversarial relationship between my clients was beginning to develop. Ernie protested that the money made from the sale of his projects was being used to support their lifestyle, and that should be enough to satisfy Joanne. I decided to try to get to the bottom of the problem as I believed it to be from the relationship we had established over the years.

I do not represent only one of them, I said, and my goal was to do my best to satisfy both Ernie and Joanne. I asked permission to ask each of them some questions. I asked Joanne what it was that she really wanted—the business assets or the security those assets represented. Security was her major concern. Did she have any objection to Ernie's son owning the business provided she was adequately taken care of if Ernie died? No, she answered. Actually, she had a great relationship with Al, and thought he had worked hard and probably deserved to take over the business. I asked Ernie if he would object to helping Al pay the premiums on a life insurance policy to fund a buyout at his death. The money would be used for Joanne's needs at Ernie's death. He did not object and Joanne thought it was the best way to resolve all of the issues. Al would get the business and Joanne her security when Ernie died. Just when I thought everything was resolved, the lawyer spoke up. "It's not that simple," he said. "Joanne needs to be compensated for the risk she has taken with her assets." It seemed to me that he was handling the situation as if Joanne and Ernie were business partners and not life partners. It also became apparent to my clients that the solution I had offered, however simple it was, would be perfect for resolving their issues, so they decided to implement it. There is no way of knowing what the outcome would have been if the lawyer persisted in making this more of a problem than it actually was. Ernie, no doubt, would have retained his own counsel and that would have probably increased the tension. In order to ensure that our clients stay on track for reaching their goals, we believe that we need to be aware of the advice they are getting from their other professionals. We communicate that to them early in the process, and most of them agree and run recommendations by us before they are implemented.

- **A Culture of Service.** Excellent, client-satisfying service that retains virtually all of your clients does not happen in a firm because the owner wills it. A culture needs to be created where *everyone* in the organization not only does what they are told, but buys into the service culture. They need to care and be proud of their jobs and be rewarded for the things that they do for clients and prospects. A securities analyst once told me that he can tell more about a company by sitting in their reception area for one day than he could from interviews with management or financial statements. He believes that a company could only be as good as its training program for its employees. If the receptionist understands the service culture of the firm, he asserts, all of its other employees certainly will.

Throughout this book, we have alluded to the importance of uncovering your clients' values to ensure that your recommendations are aligned with those values. A service culture reflects the values of a firm's owner(s) and planners. In his book, *Discovering the Soul of Service* (The Free Press, 1999), Leonard Barry writes,

> Strong institutional values enabling human beings to realize their full potential as individuals and as members of a community contribute to the creation of compelling value inside and outside the company. The company survives as a success because it is fully alive…. Values reflect what the leader holds worthy, what the organization assigns worth. They are the ideals, principles, and philosophy at the center of the enterprise. They are protected and revered. They reveal the company's heart and soul. They energize the covenant.

The people at our firm do not provide outstanding service because they have to. *They do it because they want to.*

Through their actions, all of the professionals at our firm set examples for everyone that they value service and relationships. As a result, our employees emulate them. One of the ways this is communicated is in the way we behave toward our employees. A stated core value of our firm is that we treat our employees with dignity. We deliver on all promises made, and we reward outstanding service. They are regarded as very important to our success, are respected, and they know to treat clients similarly. They also understand that no one is more important than a client is. While many service industries have forgotten the notion, we actually believe that the "customer is always right." As the analyst said, it begins with the impression people get when they call or visit.

Another planner once told me that the title for his receptionist is, "Director of First Impressions." We adopted that in our firm because it communicates to this person that her job transcends answering the phone and greeting visitors. Her job is to welcome everyone in such a way as to make them feel special, and she is successful at doing just that. We get lots of feedback from clients, as well as others, about how wonderful they feel when they call or visit. If you want this reaction in your firm, it will not happen just because you tell someone to do it. You need to create a service culture.

One of the exercises we periodically practice at our firm is to have meetings about service, which are attended by all firm personnel. We ask for any examples they may have had recently of a poor service experience. Unfortunately, in the environment in which we live today, they are not difficult to find. We then ask them what the person responsible for the misstep could have done to make the situation better. We also ask for good experiences. These meetings are just another way of reinforcing our service culture. We always tell them that mistakes will occur—we all make them. The difference between the firms that give good service and those that do not, however, is what they do after the miscue. If they handle it poorly, the client will probably remember the slip-up. If handled well, the client will remember it as a good—not bad—experience.

Recently, we discovered an error we made with a client's bonds. We had inadvertently put tax-free bonds in his IRA and taxable bonds in his taxable account. When we discovered the error, we researched what the differences would have been in taxes and income if we got it right the first time.

I called him to tell him about the error and credited his next fee by about 20 percent more than the actual loss. This turned what could have been a disaster (particularly if I had done nothing) into a positive. He thanked us for the professional manner in which we handled the situation and has referred two clients to us since that time.

It always bothers me when I need to call the owner of a company to complain that I did not get very good service from one of his employees. Invariably, the owner corrects the problem, and apologizes for the way the employee treated me. There is one major problem with firms like this and their owners. They may want their companies to provide good service (and some even delude themselves into thinking that they do), but they have failed to do something very fundamental to accomplishing good service. They failed to create a culture of service in their firms.

Advisers should not make the mistake of separating marketing and service as two separate functions in their firms. As we will discuss in another chapter, they are inextricably related. As Maister, Green, and Galford write in *The Trusted Advisor* (The Free Press, 2000), "The truth is, sales and service, when thought of properly, converge.

The two are flip sides of the same coin. And the name of that coin is acting like a trusted adviser and a caring professional."

CHAPTER 11 SUMMARY

- When providing service, think with the end in mind.
- Client retention, not marketing, is the key to growth.
- Let your clients decide how often they want to meet. Quarterly meetings may not be necessary or beneficial.
- Do not limit the services you provide if they are necessary to achieve the end result—happy and satisfied clients
- Remember that it's called financial plan*ning*. Provide your clients with periodic updates—not just investment reports.
- Be your clients' quarterback.
- The key to creating a culture of service is to communicate and demonstrate your values.

12 | *Organizing Your Firm: The Team Approach*

> *Teamwork is the ability to work together toward a common vision. The ability to direct individual accomplishments toward organizational objectives. It is the fuel that allows common people to attain uncommon results.*
>
> —Andrew Carnegie

Several years ago, I served on a panel about practice management at a national conference for financial planners. My two fellow panelists were bemoaning the amount of time they needed to accomplish all of the many tasks in their respective firms. There was little time for leisure, they complained. They saw it as the price they needed to pay for providing great service and owning a company. I disagreed.

YOUR BUSINESS IS NOT YOUR LIFE
If I counsel my clients about balancing their lives and making money their servant and not their master,

shouldn't I heed my own advice? Someone once told me not to give my clients all of my time; give them all of my good time. I do not think that is possible if I am working 60 hours a week. As Michael Gerber writes in *The E- Myth Revisited* (HarperCollins, 1995),

> …your business is not your life…. Once you recognize that the purpose of your life is not to serve your business, but the primary purpose of your business is to serve your life, you can then go to work on your business, rather than in it, with a full understanding of why it is absolutely necessary for you to do so. (Page 98)

As discussed in the previous chapter, we take client service very seriously at our firm, so reducing service in order to free up time is not acceptable. And since we have satisfied clients (as demonstrated by our retention rate), I concluded that we must be doing something right. That "something" is delegation and teamwork. We believe that involving others does much more than free up some time for our senior planners—it results in better service for our clients and valuable input from other professionals in the firm. As Ken Blanchard has said, "None of us is as smart as all of us." It also creates a clear career path for new planners and results in future growth.

THE PROFESSIONAL PRACTICE MODEL

Many financial planners, including me, got their starts in product sales and the organizations they have created may not reflect the reality and dynamics of a professional planning firm, which are considerably different from a sales organization. In the latter, the primary skill one looks for when hiring people (other than support staff) is sales ability. New associates are required and expected to bring new clients to the firm almost immediately. Their training is more sales- than service-oriented. On the other hand, professional practices like accounting and law seek bright, technically competent individuals who can help the firm serve its clients. As more business is brought to the firm from its rainmakers, associates are hired to work with these clients. Those associates who have the inclination and ability to attract new clients are encouraged to do so, and eventually may become partners or shareholders. This is a model that I believe will serve financial planning firms.

When I was president of FPA and conducted discussion groups around the country on the future of the profession, one of the questions we posed to FPA members was, "Have you ever hired any professionals in your firm?" Some hands would be raised and our follow-up question was, "Tell us how it worked for you." Invariably, someone would tell us that it did not work because, "they didn't bring in any new business." They were operating under the old sales organization model, one that is not conducive to building a professional firm. Many others expressed concern about the amount of money they needed to pay "unproductive people." The problem, as I see it, is that many of these planners do not understand the dynamics of building a business. In the last chapter, we quoted Stephen Covey, "Begin with the end in mind." If your goal is to build a successful business, that takes both time and money. A businessperson views the salaries of competent associates as an investment. The planner who is reluctant to do so sees them as an expense. If your idea of an idyllic life is to have your practice become your life with no relief in sight (as Gerber says, you will become a victim of your success), do not make that investment. I decided early in my career that I wanted to build a firm that could function without me. To do so meant investing in quality people. As far as "training my competitors," so be it. We are interested in having competent people in our firm to serve our clients. If they should decide to open their own firms, that is fine—after all, that was *my* goal. However, the valuable people we have hired in our firm have not left because we have made it possible for them to acquire ownership positions. Once again, law and accounting firms have done quite well by offering ownership opportunities to their associates who are able to attract new clients to their firms. Another benefit of offering ownership opportunities is that these shareholders can serve as your management staff.

SHAREHOLDERS' RESPONSIBILITIES

I cannot imagine how a firm could grow into a viable business if one person is responsible for obtaining clients, compliance, operations, finance, client meetings, organizing agendas, financial planning, ongoing service, investment policy, researching investments, and all of the other functions that need attention in order to be profitable. As Mark Tibergien has observed to financial planners, "Look for a COO and other members of your operations team from within. If you don't have staff that can tackle these posts, turn to recruiters and the Web. But don't delay." Those who do so are flourishing. SmartPros, Ltd., referring to the *2004 FPA Financial Performance Study* conducted by Moss Adams, wrote, "The gap between the top 25 percent of firms and the other 75 percent of firms is widening, the study shows.

Owners in the top 25 percent are taking home over $250,000 more per year than their peers." As a small firm (we have 12 employees, including professionals), each shareholder takes on the responsibility of managing various functions. How you organize your firm will depend on several factors. However, the functions listed need to be performed by any firm that practices financial life planning.

- **Chief Operations Officer**
  We have followed Mark Tibergien's advice and appointed one of our shareholders to serve as our COO. He is not primarily responsible for attracting new clients and he is not on a financial planning team (see below). Therefore, he has time to devote to running the day-to-day operations. This is not and should not be a part-time job, but it will be if a sole proprietor insists on doing it herself. He also is responsible for compliance, a daunting task, as we all know. As a result, our operations run very smoothly and the planners in our firm have the time to concentrate on activities that are most productive, such as serving existing and attracting new clients.
- **Director of Financial Planning**
  His duties include:
  - Coordinating the efforts of our teams to ensure that what everyone delivers to all of our clients is consistent. While we certainly do not produce "cookie cutter" plans, we need to make sure that the layout is similar and all of our clients receive the same basic information, such as cash flow and tax projections, estate planning, insurance needs analyses, etc.
  - Reviewing planning software and making recommendations to add or change vendors

–Serving as chairman of our financial planning committee

–Working closely with the director of investments, ensuring that the assumptions used for investment returns are compatible with our investment policies

While each planner has a great deal of flexibility in presenting plans, we never forget that we are building a firm, not an ensemble of several independent planners. Knowing that we have someone who is ultimately responsible for coordinating our financial planning efforts frees time for other planners to concentrate on their responsibilities. For example, if one of us receives information about a product or vendor that we feel needs to be pursued, we give it to our director for review. We have faith in his ability to evaluate opportunities, so we do not need to duplicate our efforts. There have been situations when a planner has asked our director to review a program only to learn that it was looked at several weeks earlier.

- **Director of Investments**

In addition to serving as chairman of our investment committee, this shareholder coordinates all firm investment activities. Among his responsibilities are:

–Ensuring that trades are made promptly and accurately

–Reviewing the performance of our investments and suggesting changes to the committee when he feels it is appropriate

–Researching investments

–Selecting bonds for each client's portfolio that are compatible with instructions he receives from planners

–Quarterly performance reporting

–Investment database management

–Reviewing and recommending investment software

–Keeping our investment policy statements up-to-date

- Communicating investment policy changes to all firm associates
- **Director of Qualified Plans**
  Duties and responsibilities:
  - Keeping abreast of all law changes and communicating them to all associates
  - Reviewing and selecting retirement plan products, custodians, and third-party administrators, as well as acting as liaison for the firm
  - Reviewing new and existing clients' qualified retirement plans and making recommendations for improvements
  - Conducting educational meetings for employees of firms where we have installed 401(k) plans
  - Preparation of 5500 EZ forms for our clients who have one-person plans
  - Meeting with clients about their plans when necessary
- **Finance Director**
  No company will continue to serve clients if it is not profitable, so we believe that a senior shareholder should handle finances. The duties of this director include:
  - Acting as liaison with our bookkeeping/payroll service (we have chosen to outsource these functions)
  - Budgeting and forecasting
  - Providing shareholders with quarterly financial progress reports.
  - Approving requests for expenditures not budgeted

FINANCIAL PLANNING TEAMS

I am a great believer in synergy—that the whole is greater than the sum of its parts. We have applied that to our team-building, and the results truly demonstrate the reality of that statement. Financial life planning, when practiced correctly, is very labor intensive. Without teams, it would be impossible for us to complete the intensive discovery process, prepare detailed recommendations and reports, periodically update clients' situations, invest and rebalance portfolios, provide prompt answers to clients' questions and concerns, research the data necessary to give up-to-date advice, and provide our clients with the quality service we discussed. Our financial life planning teams consist of three associates: a senior planner, an associate planner, and an administrative assistant. The head of the team (senior planner) is a shareholder and a CFP practitioner, as is the associate planner. The administrative assistant may hold a certificate in paraplanning. The general duties of each are:

- **Senior Planner**
  - Leading the team
  - Getting business for the team (the rainmaker)
  - Conducting all qualitative discovery meetings
  - Making and/or approving all planning recommendations
  - Helping the clients choose an investment policy
  - Being the primary relationship manager for clients assigned to the team
- **Associate Planner**
  - Attending all client meetings
  - Taking notes at client meetings
  - Data entry in our financial planning software (we believe that this is not a job for a paraplanner, because more than a basic knowledge is necessary to produce technically accurate plans)
  - Preparing all financial planning reports from preliminary to final, including all updates

– Interacting with clients to update information as well as to answer basic questions they may have
– Working closely with the senior planner and keeping him informed of issues and progress of all clients
– Coordinating paperwork, such as the opening of accounts, with the administrative assistant
– Preparing the agenda for each client's meeting
– Preparing investment policy statements for senior planners' reviews
– Preparing initial and portfolio rebalancing recommendations for senior planners' reviews

- **Administrative Assistant**
  – Working closely with other team members
  – Scheduling all appointments
  – Preparing paperwork to open and transfer accounts
  – Tracking the transfer of assets and informing other team members when accounts are ready to invest
  – Coordinating with custodians
  – Facilitating clients' scheduled and nonscheduled withdrawals
  – Tracking available cash for clients who are withdrawing and informing team members when cash needs replenishing
  – Returning and/or handling all calls from clients when other team members are not available
  – Performing other administrative duties as required

Our clients realize that several people in our firm are available to serve their needs. As a result, they bypass the senior planner for most of their needs. In addition to our team members, other associates in the firm are available to help all clients. No one in our firm will ever proclaim, "That is not my job!" The culture of service we discussed before is evident in the attitudes of all of our associates, and they take pride when clients and planners compliment them on the great work that they do.

COMMITTEES

We have committees for the following: financial planning, investments, finance, compliance, and qualified retirement plans. One of our shareholders chairs each committee and others in the firm may serve as committee members. We believe they are very important for several reasons. First, they clearly assign responsibility for each specific function to the appropriate committee chair. This frees the rest of the people in the firm to concentrate on their own responsibilities. Second, the fact that at least three associates serve on each committee employs the principle that "none of us is as smart as all of us." We make no major decisions without committee involvement. And, perhaps most important, it gives us an opportunity to involve more associates in the decision-making process.

CAREER PATHS

I once read an article written by a recent graduate with a degree in financial planning from a well-respected university. He had passed his CFP exam and was looking for an entry-level position with a financial planning firm. He was lamenting about how difficult it was to find what he was looking for. He was willing to relocate, but, as he wrote, "the pickings were slim." When he was offered positions, most of them were in product sales, which did not interest him. When he did get that rare offer from a firm that practiced financial planning, it was for a salary that was almost minimum wage with no benefits. As I read that article, I asked myself, "Is this any way to build a profession?" If we are to flourish in this relatively new profession of financial planning, it will only be done one firm at a time. Why are planners who advise their clients about the future so reluctant to invest in their own futures? Who will our future planners be, if not these newly-minted financial planning graduates? Moreover, what will happen to our firms? Will they no longer exist when the owner/principal retires or dies? We need a career path, not only for the development of our profession, but also for the preservation and growth of our firms.

We believe our team structure provides opportunities for young planners, valuable assistance for us, and the prospect for these associates to become senior planners and shareholders in our firm. The entry-level position for people who have passed the CFP exam or are in the program is associate planner. The duties are described above, and as you review them, you will notice that sales is not one of their responsibilities. They will pay for themselves (and we offer them a competitive starting salary) by freeing up time for senior planners to attract more new clients. Once they are familiar with our process and have developed strong client-relationship skills (it takes at least two years), they are encouraged, but not required, to bring new business to the firm. We support their efforts to do so. If they are successful, we will offer them an opportunity to buy shares in the firm and develop their own teams. And the cycle begins again. As a result, we are able to attract quality people and the firm continues to grow.

While financial life planning may be your passion and the purpose of your existence, you must never lose sight of the notion that you are building a business. It is not the nature of human beings to remain static. You must either grow or regress. Your firm and its organizational structure should reflect the fact that you have chosen growth.

CHAPTER 12 SUMMARY

- The primary purpose of your business is to serve your life.
- Financial planning is a profession. Organize your firm as a professional practice.
- You will be rewarded by investing time and money in your firm.
- Appoint specialists to be responsible for the functions in your practice, such as investing, finance, and operations.
- Since "none of us is as smart as all of us," create committees.
- Develop a career path for your associates that rewards them for remaining with your firm by offering ownership opportunities.
- Financial planning teams improve efficiency, client service, and facilitate the growth of your firm.

13 Getting Your Staff on Board: Motivating and Compensating

It is literally true that you can succeed best and quickest by helping others to succeed.

—Napoleon Hill

Many years ago, when I was a regional vice president for a major insurance company, I appointed a new general agent to manage an office in my territory. Among the people he inherited was a very qualified office manager who had been with the company for over 30 years. Shortly after his appointment, he decided that he would rearrange the furniture in the administrative area. He did so on a Saturday, when the office was closed. That Monday, his office manager discovered what this new general agent had done without consulting her. She came to the conclusion that she did not want to work for anyone who did not respect her. This was her area of accountability, and she felt that he had no right to unilaterally change the work space for which she was responsible. I am sure that he believed that it was a more efficient layout, and he may have even convinced her, *if he had consulted her*. He didn't and she resigned. He learned a valuable lesson about how to treat employees that day.

Employees are much more conscientious than many employers give them credit for. Does anyone really believe that there are people who show up for work in the morning with the intention of doing a poor job? Then why are so many employers so quick to criticize their associates when they do not perform up to their expectations? It is probably valid that happy employees perform better than unhappy ones. However, it is also true that good job performance is a factor in happiness. It is a rare person, indeed, who gets no satisfaction from performing well. So what comes first—happiness or job excellence? I'm not sure, but I do know that the only thing we have some control over is how the people we hire perform. Moreover, there are only two basic reasons that employees do not excel: either they do not possess the necessary skills for the job they are in, or they were not trained properly. And since we control both, how far do we need to look to assess fault? Only when we recognize that the trouble (if we have any) is the direct result of either something we have done (hiring the wrong person) or something we have not done (training), can we correct the problem.

SELECT THE RIGHT PEOPLE

I once heard an executive from Nordstrom's department store (known for their world-class service) say that his company has a rigorous training program for all of their employees that stresses customer service. However, in spite of this education, some people never perform up to Nordstrom's standards and need to be let go. He said, in order to survive in their environment, employees must really like people, and Nordstrom's has not discovered a selection tool that accurately predicts that. Once they discover that an employee doesn't really like people, there is no amount of training that can correct the problem. Therefore, selecting the right people for your firm is the first logical step in building a team that is service-oriented and reflects your values. For us, like Nordstrom's, it is imperative that everyone we hire possess strong relationship skills, since all of them will have client contact from time to time. If we are satisfied with the training we provided, when we discover that someone is not treating clients and other associates properly, we replace them.

While we have not yet discovered a selection tool that definitely measures how employees will react to clients, there are clues you will get during the interview process. People with good relationship skills are usually very personable and well liked. As long as they possess the necessary technical skills for the positions we are filling, we tend to hire people that we like. This may not seem very scientific, but most of the time it has resulted in employees who have good people skills and fit very well in the culture we have created in our firm. After all, if Nordstrom's hasn't been hasn't been able to discover a selection tool that predicts how employees will act toward their customers, we must conclude that such a method does not exist. However, our "gut feelings" about people have served us well over the years. It may only be anecdotal evidence, but our experiences have taught us that people who like other people want to be liked themselves, and they demonstrate that during the interview process.

CREATING A SUCCESSFUL ENVIRONMENT

Eisenhower once defined leadership as, "the art of getting someone else to do something you want done because he wants to do it." When I began a career in the life insurance business many years ago, my general agent and mentor, who had an agency full of motivated people, taught me a valuable lesson about motivation. He told me that no human being possesses the skills to keep people motivated for long periods. A good coach, he told me, may be able to get his players "up" for an important game, but cannot sustain that kind of motivation throughout a season. When I questioned why some coaches and successful businesspeople seem to have more than their share of motivated people in their organizations, he told me there were two reasons for that. First, he said, they selected good people who were self-motivated (see above). However, the most important skill these extraordinary leaders possess is the ability to create environments that are conducive to success. It answers the question of why some mediocre people thrive when they change jobs or teams. Years ago, much of the success of the New York Yankees was just "wearing the Yankee pinstripes." It wasn't the uniform—it was the environment created by management that made the difference. These players did not obtain superior pitching or hitting skills when they joined their new team. But they were in an environment that was more conducive to success. My mentor also told me that while it is not possible to motivate individuals, managers certainly have the ability to de-motivate them.

NONMONETARY REWARDS

While we do have monetary incentives for virtually all of our employees (see below), we strongly believe that money is not the primary motivator for employee performance. If we are to create and sustain that "Yankee pinstripe" environment that is conducive to success, we need to do more than just pay them well. We need to develop a work environment that our associates enjoy coming to each morning—a place that brings out the best in them. There are several things that you can do to accomplish this:

- **Practice what you preach.** You cannot tell your employees that clients and others must be treated with respect and dignity if you do not treat them with respect and dignity. When you create an environment that is built on mutual respect and dignity, associates do not need constant reminders of how important those qualities are. We do not tolerate, for example, clients who are abusive to our employees. Moreover, we are willing to lose revenue in order to adhere to this core value of ours. Not too long ago, a new client who was paying us a retainer of $12,000 per year was criticizing a team member for something she had failed to do, according to the client. I called the client and discussed the problem with her (the employee was actually following my instructions) and requested that, in the future, if she had issues with any of our employees, she tell me about them and not vent to the employees. She basically told me that she would do as she pleased since she was paying us. I politely asked her to find another adviser. The important thing about this incident and others like it is that our associates know that we value them and their dignity. When necessary, we are willing to sacrifice revenue to prove it.

- **Praise publicly.** Who among us does not want to be told when we are doing a good job? We need to be very generous with our praise, because people want to know when they are appreciated. The first time a Microsoft programmer got a congratulatory e-mail from Bill Gates, he printed it and framed it. This may seem obvious, but so many of us go about our day and take the things our employees do for our clients and us for granted. I once had a person tell me, "That's what I pay them to do!" Of course it is, but there are many others firms who are willing to pay just as much or more for their services. The theme of this book is that people's lives, not their money, are most important to them. Of course, your compensation needs to be competitive. However, employees normally don't leave because they are looking for more money. They look for new jobs when they are unhappy, and not being appreciated is a major cause of job dissatisfaction. When members of my financial planning team are out sick, they usually call to make sure that items that require attention are taken care of in their absence. They feel like vital parts of our organization, which they are, and we cannot tell them enough how much we appreciate all they do. Our clients give us positive feedback on how they are treated and we make sure that everyone in our organization knows about it each time it happens.
- **Educate on the value of financial life planning.** Is it enough to train a receptionist on how to answer phones and greet people? We think it is not. If we expect all our employees and associates to understand the value we bring to our clients, we need to educate them. Our administrative assistants on our financial planning teams are encouraged to take the CFP course in paraplanning.

They are involved in the recommendations we make. It is not enough, for example, to instruct someone to change a client's account from "joint with right of survivorship" to "tenants in common." We want them to understand the reasons for doing so. They are taught about RMDs (required minimum distributions) so that they are aware of why we are doing what we are doing each year, and how the amount is calculated. A basic understanding of income taxes will raise a flag when a client calls and requests money from her IRA when there is sufficient cash available from other sources and a RMD is not necessary. Educating our employees on the financial planning process, of course, helps us to be more efficient and reduces the likelihood of error. But it also helps to make them feel like the integral parts of the firm that they are. We give them a great deal of responsibility and they know that we trust them to do good work. To paraphrase Abraham Lincoln, if you look for good in people expecting to find it, you surely will.

- **Create a "family" atmosphere.** If a person is to spend almost half of the time they are awake on the job, it should be as much fun as it prudently can be. We strongly believe that at our firm, and we do whatever we can to make them feel a part of our "family." I have read books on management that criticize that description for a business. An enterprise with a profit motive, they tell us, is a serious matter. A family atmosphere can be too casual and produce unwanted results, they warn. Nothing could be further from the truth at our firm. As we wrote in an earlier chapter, our employees do not address clients by their first names without being invited to do so. We are all business, but why can't business be fun? We do our best to ensure that our firm is a pleasant place to work, and we all genuinely like each other. Our employees refer to our firm's "family" atmosphere without coaching from us. Several years ago, we had a receptionist leave because she moved to Delaware and the commute was very difficult for her (she had a young son). She stays in touch with us through e-mails and telephone calls. She tells us how much she misses the "family." She was a very valued employee we did not want to lose. She made our clients feel at home each time she had contact with them because she felt at home at her job. As we mentioned earlier, happy employees perform better. It is our job as managers to create the atmosphere that makes it possible.

COMPENSATING PROFESSIONALS AND STAFF

The amount you pay your staff and professionals is unique to your area, so the only thing I will mention about how much you pay your people is that it needs to be competitive. While compensation may not be the overriding factor in attracting and keeping associates, you cannot expect to pay considerably less than the competition and have competent people join your firm. Enough about the amount you pay. This section will discuss the way we structure our compensation for associates and shareholders.

- **Our compensation philosophy.** We believe that, whenever possible, associates should be rewarded for the contributions they make to the overall growth of the firm. While this may be difficult to quantify for some employees, it is easier for team members and professionals who bring new clients to the firm. We don't believe in "eating your own kill," because that is a compensation system that may result in unhealthy competition among associates. While the base salaries we pay are the largest part of our associates' compensation, our incentive compensation programs provide rewards for growth.

- **Team members' compensation.** Since all of our team leaders are also shareholders, we will cover their compensation later. As we discussed in the chapter on organization, our teams comprise an associate planner and an administrative assistant, in addition to the senior planner (team leader). While I am not suggesting that you adopt the same percentages we do, the concept is one that you may want to consider. It has worked very well for us and has virtually eliminated the need for salary increase discussions each year. Each of our associate planners receives a base salary plus 4 percent of all revenue generated by the team on which he serves. The team administrative assistant gets a base salary plus 1.5 percent of team revenue. While their incentive income is not the major part of their compensation, it provides everyone on the team with a direct reward for getting and keeping clients.

- **Shareholder/team leaders' compensation.** Our chapter on organization covered our departments and committee structures. Each shareholder is expected to serve as a department head as well as a leader and business generator for his/her team. In addition to the base salary that is paid to all shareholders, the firm pays an additional salary for these other duties. The total paid for these additional duties is based on the amount of work they require. Team leaders are also paid an incentive of 15 percent of the fees generated by their teams. As you can see, everyone on the team shares in the success of the team, and this helps facilitate cooperation and efficiency. We are an "S" corporation, so shareholders also receive their shares of distributable profit each year.

- **Chief Operating Officer compensation.** Since our COO/shareholder does not lead a team and is not primarily responsible for bringing new business to the firm, his compensation is somewhat different. In addition to his base salary, he receives 4 percent of revenue generated by the *entire* firm. He performs a valuable function and frees up time for the rest of us to do what we do best—attract and serve clients.
- **Subjective bonuses.** In addition to the incentive compensation, the shareholders may elect to pay bonuses to associates who may have done extraordinary jobs, and we do that occasionally. However, the incentives we pay are designed to take much of the subjectivity out of paying special compensation. There are employees who do not receive incentives, such as our receptionist; so subjective bonuses are needed from time to time to reward employees not assigned to a specific team.

OWNERSHIP OPPORTUNITIES

As I look back on my career in financial planning and the development of the firm, I can say unequivocally that the best decision I made was to invite key associates to buy shares in the firm and become partners. No other decision has had the same impact on our growth over the years. We have had unusual stability (three of us have been with the firm for over 20 years). When we hire new associates, they join us with the full knowledge that they can become shareholders when they reach predetermined targets. In fact, we have added two new shareholders in the past three years. We intend to continue that trend. Our system for buying shares is simple. We value the company internally, as a multiple of gross revenue. You may settle on a different formula or even get a professional appraisal to value your firm. We chose simplicity, but it is the concept—not the formula—that is important. New shareholders are initially offered an opportunity to buy 5 percent of the company. As they continue to progress, more shares will be offered to them. If they choose to do so, the company will finance the purchase over five years at market interest rates. Our experience has demonstrated that their distributions and additional shareholder income will exceed their annual payments (if they extend the payments) after two years. While we are not equal shareholders (I still own the majority of the outstanding shares, though not by design), none of us has ever voted our shares. At meetings, we each have one vote, and that has made for a very healthy relationship among us. There are other significant advantages:

- We each have a market for the shares we own. We have exercised a stock-redemption plan that will assure us a fair value for our shares in the event of death, disability, or retirement.
- We have learned from each other over the years, because of the broadened perspective that comes from having multiple owners.
- Good people do not leave the firm to establish their own practices.
- Key duties are shared by all owners and are not left for one person to accomplish.
- The incentive to grow the firm is intense.
- Recruiting quality associates is enhanced.

I once heard the story of a man who was charged with building a tunnel through a mountain. He instructed half of his employees to start digging on one side of the mountain. The other half was told to dig toward the first group. He proclaimed, "If we meet, we have a tunnel. If we don't, we have two tunnels." We want one tunnel, and a sure way of accomplishing that goal is to be certain that your employees are on the same page by selecting, motivating, and compensating them properly.

CHAPTER 13 SUMMARY
- Happy employees perform well.
- Select people with good relationship skills.
- Employees cannot be taught to like people.
- Leaders need to create an environment where motivated people thrive.
- Treat your employees with dignity.
- Educate all of your employees on the value of financial planning.
- Provide monetary rewards for growth.
- Offer exceptional associates ownership opportunities.

14 | *The Value of Advice: A Fee Structure for Financial Life Planners*

A cynic is a man who knows the price of everything, and the value of nothing.

—Oscar Wilde

Imagine yourself visiting a physician who tells you the following: "If you will hire me as your primary doctor, I will diagnose all of your illnesses, treat you when you are ill, help you with your dieting, recommend a program for preventative care, prescribe any drugs you may need, monitor your progress, refer you to competent specialists when needed, and be available to help you with any questions or concerns you may have about your health. In short, I will be your personal medical adviser." Upon hearing this, you may be overwhelmed and believe that this is too good to be true in this age of managed care, but you ask the obvious question, "How much will this cost?" The doctor replies, "All you need to do is buy the drugs from me."

Now how are you feeling? What are some of the thoughts running through your head? What has the doctor communicated is the most important thing he does? Are you concerned that he will be compelled to prescribe drugs in order to be paid? Are you worried that you may not need these drugs? Would you rather pay him a retainer for his medical advice if he will let you buy the drugs on your own? Of course, doctors no longer sell drugs and they are paid for their core competencies—their ability to diagnose and treat illnesses. Why should financial planning be any different? Why do we earn most of our compensation from the commodities we offer instead of for the most valuable services and advice we give? Moreover, if you would not want to pay for medical advice in this manner, why should paying for financial advice be different for clients of financial planners? Doesn't everyone crave conflict-free advice? We do so much for our clients, and our experience has taught us that they value the services of financial life planners and are willing to pay for those services.

THE IMPORTANT WORK WE DO

If you were to list what you do for your clients, how would you rank them in importance?

- Discovering your clients' needs and goals (performing the physical)
- Analyzing their current situation and determining if there will be shortfalls (diagnosing the illness)
- Recommending financially viable solutions (prescribing the treatment)
- Helping them implement the recommendations (treating the patient)

- Monitoring their progress (annual physicals)
- Building a portfolio (prescribing drugs)
- Implementing investment decisions (buying the drugs)

I would postulate that the least important service listed is implementing the investments, yet that is still how most financial planners are paid. Some planners I know have actually told me that financial planning is a "loss leader." How can the most important service we provide—our core competency—be something we lose money on, while the commodity we offer (investment management) be the primary source of our income? If financial life planning is to become the respected profession I know it can be, we need to be paid for the most important thing we bring to every relationship—our wisdom. Our clients can find and implement investments on the Internet, but they will never find the wisdom of a competent and caring financial planner who can make the difference between financial success and failure for so many people. Moreover, the financial life planning approach and services we have discussed in this book are unique, and clients are willing to pay for them. As Harvard Business School professor Theodore Levitt said, "People don't want to buy a quarter-inch drill. They want a quarter-inch hole." Too many planners are selling the drill (products and money management) and not the hole (financial peace of mind).

FEE SCHEDULES THAT REFLECT VALUE

The fee schedules for financial life planning firms need to reflect the relative value of what they do. And charging a one-time fee for a "plan" is not good enough. We do *planning*, which presumes that it is ongoing, and "throwing it in for free" as long as we are managing the assets will not persuade our clients to value the advice we give as more important than anything we do. Many planners I have interviewed have told me that they would like to change their fee schedules but are concerned that clients would not be willing to pay fees that are not based on assets managed. Actually, we felt this way in our firm for some time. In speeches I would give at financial adviser meetings, I would predict that retainers would become the norm for our profession of financial life planning. Invariably, I would be asked if I had implemented such a fee schedule at our firm. I would answer, "Not yet." I feared that my clients were not ready for such a change, so I continued to charge a percentage of the assets I managed and communicated that it was really a retainer for all of the services we offered. Unfortunately, if you are paid for the assets, your clients will probably perceive that to be the most important service you provide. Remember how you felt when the doctor wanted to be paid for the drugs and not his advice? What did his method of charging his patients communicate what his most important service/product was?

I was asked the same question at the FPA annual conference in New Orleans in 2002. "Have you implemented it in your firm?" Embarrassed by my usual response, this time my answer changed. "I have not, but I intend to do so for all new clients when I return." When I returned to the office, I asked my partners if I could add a flat retainer fee to our ADV. They could continue to charge asset management fees, but I did not wish to do so. They agreed. My results actually exceeded my expectations, and my fears were totally unjustified. When the other shareholders observed the results of this new fee schedule and the favorable response of new clients, they decided to implement it for the entire firm within six months.

ESSENTIAL INGREDIENTS IN A FEE SCHEDULE

There are many ways a financial planning firm can charge fees, and I am not suggesting that the flat retainers we have implemented in our firm are ideal for everyone. However, it works very well for us and you may want to consider it. To me, a fee schedule needs to have the following to be successful:

- **It must result in a profit.** This may seem obvious, and it should be. Financial life planning, as we have discussed, is very labor-intensive and needs to be reflected in your fee schedule. We will not be discussing the amount of fees to charge because there are many variables that are part of that determination. In addition to being sufficient to ensure firm profitability, your fees must also be competitive for what you offer. Always remember when determining how much to charge for your services, that price resistance is really value resistance. The amount a client is willing to pay will be directly related to the value that client perceives she will receive. The financial life planning services outlined in this book will be highly valued and, as we have mentioned before, clients are willing to pay for them.
- **It needs to reflect the importance of the various services you provide.** This is my major objection to asset-based fees. I have repeated throughout this book that asset management is a highly overrated commodity. I acknowledge its importance in providing peace of mind for our clients, but so many other things we do are much more valuable. Review the list of services that we developed earlier in

this chapter. Is implementing investments more important than discovering a client's most important goals? Or recommending viable solutions? How about monitoring progress and staying up-to-date on important changes in our clients' lives? If the only fees we charge are for the assets we manage, regardless of whether we communicate that to be a "financial planning retainer" (as we once did), our clients will perceive that as our most important service. For money managers it is. But we are financial life planners, and we want our fee schedule to make a different statement. You may want to consider a base retainer and a smaller asset management fee. If you do, I would structure your schedule in such a way that the asset management portion is always smaller than the flat retainers are. Many planners may choose to bill hourly. While I do not object to charging hourly fees, remember that you communicate by doing so that your time is your most important commodity. I recall the story about a woman who noticed Pablo Picasso in a restaurant. She approached him and asked if he would be kind enough to draw a sketch on her napkin. He did so, but when she reached for it, Mr. Picasso pulled it away and said, "That will be $5,000." "What do you mean?" she protested. "That only took you five minutes." "No," he answered, "that took me 50 years!" In my opinion, we offer valuable, almost priceless advice. How long it takes me to solve a problem or make a competent recommendation is not relevant to your clients. They are looking for solutions and results. In fact, the more proficient you become, the less time it may take you to offer good advice. Under the hourly model, you may be paid less for being competent, knowledgeable, and efficient.

- **It should be easy to understand and communicate to clients.** When we first started to offer financial planning on a fee basis, we attempted to have a fee schedule that reflected almost every contingency. It was so complicated that none of us could ever memorize it. Clients certainly did not understand it and it was difficult to tell prospects what their fee would be without us collecting much data. Asset management fees have the advantage of being easy to understand. Most people understand hourly fees, but it may be difficult to estimate what a client's fee will be in advance. We used to charge hourly fees and found that keeping track of hours was not a productive use of our time. Our flat retainers are very easy to understand and communicate. Clients are told what the fee will be and that it covers all services we perform.
- **It should pay you for what you can control.** When discussing the advantages of a flat retainer over asset-based fees, I often ask prospective clients the following questions. "What if I am managing your portfolio and the market increases by 20 percent in one year. Your portfolio experiences a similar increase. What have I done to change the market?" She will answer, "Nothing." "Then why should you give me a raise for something over which I had no control? Let's assume the other scenario. The market and your portfolio both lose 10 percent in a year. I also did nothing to cause that. Why should you reduce the fee you pay me? In fact, we have discovered that we are more valuable when the markets are not doing well because we will help you to avoid the mistakes many people make at those times. I want to be judged and paid for things I can control, such as being relentless in discovering what is important to you, responding to your requests quickly and

accurately, giving you competent advice that matches your goals, keeping your planning up to date, etc. Compensating me for portfolio volatility is not fair to you or me."

OUR APPROACH TO FEES

As discussed, the amount of the fees each firm charges is unique to that firm, where it is located, and other variables. At our firm, we calculate our retainer fees based loosely on net worth. For example, if a client's net worth is less than $1 million, his annual retainer fee would be X (the base fee). For each additional $500,000 of net worth, the base fee would increase by Y. Fees are paid quarterly and include all of the services of the firm. There are no additional fees for the initial discovery and planning process. Retainer clients are not billed additionally for anything they may need or request. This knowledge encourages them to call us. The initial fee is not adjusted for three years, regardless of the client's situation. We have made a decision in our firm that we do not want to have an annual discussion about fees with our clients. Moreover, they know that their fees are not affected by additional money they may acquire or for withdrawals. There are several advantages of charging flat retainers:

- **It significantly reduces conflicts of interest.** While it may be impossible to eliminate conflicts, flat fees certainly do reduce them. We tell prospective clients this by using the following example. "Assume we charged a percentage of assets managed (let's assume 1 percent) and you approached us with an opportunity to invest $500,000 in a small business. You would like our advice on this venture, which would require taking the money from the portfolio we manage. Obviously, we can give two possible answers. If we tell you that we believe it would not be in your best interests to invest this money, would you find that advice, regardless of how sincere it was, to be tainted because we would lose $5,000 of revenue if you made the investment? On the other hand, we could advise you to withdraw the money from the portfolio and make the investment. In that case, the result of the good advice we have given will cost us $5,000 in fees. Our system eliminates that conflict." Recently, a prospective client who was retiring interviewed several financial planners. When he came to see me, he informed me that he had made a tentative decision to take a monthly pension in lieu of a lump sum, but still had time to change his mind. He was not ready to make a decision about a financial adviser, but asked if I would object to reviewing his election. I agreed and the monthly income seemed quite generous when compared with the lump sum, so I informed him that I thought he made a good decision. Several days later, he called me to tell me that his wife was very concerned. One of the financial advisers they interviewed told them that taking a lump sum was a better option for them. His wife asked him to call me to determine if they were correct in taking the monthly income. I reassured him and he told me, "That's what I thought you would say. I guess the reason they want me to take the lump sum is because their fees are based on a percentage of assets." I have no idea whether the fee he would have gotten with his recommendation motivated that other planner. He may have sincerely believed that it was in the client's best interest to take the lump sum. I do know, however, that the prospective client believed that the conflict affected the planner's recommendation. (They hired our firm.)

- **The emphasis is on the advice, not the asset management.** We have repeated this several times, but when the fee is a percentage of the portfolio, the client perceives the portfolio to be the client. We have discovered that clients value and appreciate the other services we provide because they know that is what they are paying us for. Client meetings are not dominated by discussions of their investment portfolios. If fact, other issues, such as charitable giving, future plans, travel, purchasing a second home, educating children and grandchildren, plans for the coming years, short- and long-term goals, are what are regularly covered at these meetings. We used to tell clients that our asset management fees were actually retainers for all of our services, but it did not send that message clearly enough.
- **People will more readily give you their assets to manage.** When clients understand that they will pay no more for turning their assets over to us to manage, they are more likely to do so. While I do not want to give anyone the impression that managing portfolios is the most important service we provide, it is important that we have control over as much of their investments as possible. In Chapter 7, we demonstrated the mistakes clients make when they do it themselves. When other brokers/money managers are investing our clients' money, they may not be in harmony with what we want to accomplish. It is much easier for our firm to manage the assets than to monitor what others may be doing. Recently, a client told us that he wanted to keep about half of his portfolio with a broker he had known for many years. We evaluated the job this person was doing

and felt that our client would be better off if we managed the assets to ensure that the investment policy was compatible with his goals. The knowledge that this recommendation was not motivated by our desire to collect more fees made a difference and the portfolio was transferred to our control.

- **Administrative simplicity.** We still have clients we have not converted to flat retainers (many have been clients for ten or more years), but for our retainer clients, the simplicity of billing the same amount each quarter has been welcomed by our administrative staff. We only need to follow up with clients regarding their fees every three years to recalculate them. It is a simple system for our clients and for us. In addition, budgeting becomes more predictable and is not dependent on the whims of the market.

We have been charging flat retainers for our new clients since 2002, and we will never return to the old system. We have discovered a system that our clients like. One person actually told us that he always wanted to pay a flat fee but everyone he visited wanted to charge a percentage of assets. People crave conflict-free advice in this time of corporate corruption, conflicted analysts, and mutual fund scandals, and a flat fee arrangement seems to be "just what the doctor ordered." More important, our clients' focus is on the total advice we give, because that is what they are paying for. And we do not need to manage assets in order to be paid. If we encounter a business owner who has invested all of her money in her business but needs ongoing financial advice, we can accommodate her because we have no minimum investment amount in order to be a client.

A planner once asked me if I thought I should be paid more if my clients did well, and I answered that I did. He then asked how that could be done without charging a percentage of assets. I replied, "You just defined 'doing well' as growing the portfolio. I define it differently. Doing well to me means that clients are reaching their goals, their money is aligned with their lives, they have peace of mind through volatile markets, they know that someone is looking out for their financial interests, and they have a relationship that is built on trust and not returns. Perhaps doing well was not agonizing over the 30-month market turndown from 2000 to 2002. As discussed above, I believe that we should be paid for what we can control. Since we have no control over the markets, we don't deserve huge increases when they do well, nor should we take a reduction in income when they do not. Our new retainer clients agree with that.

Any time a group of financial planners gets together, one of the subjects that seems to be discussed is how we can be recognized as a profession. One answer would be to start thinking of ourselves as professionals who understand and believe in the value of our advice—so much so that we are willing to charge reasonable fees for it and not camouflage it in asset management fees. Most consumers perceive financial planning as "managing money," and we are partially to blame for that.

If we are serious about building this profession, we need to act as other professionals and be paid for the value we bring to each relationship. We need to stop the practice of earning most of our money from the commodities we implement and begin being paid for the wisdom and advice we provide.

CHAPTER 14 SUMMARY

- Your fee schedule needs to reflect the value of your advice.
- Charging asset management fees for all services may send the wrong message to your clients.
- Make a list of the services you provide and rank them in importance. Your fee schedule should reflect your rankings.
- Contrary to the opinions of many financial planners, clients are willing to pay fees that are not based entirely on assets under management, and they're willing to pay fees for the advice they receive.
- A fee schedule should contain the following elements:
  - It must result in a profit.
  - It should reflect the relative importance of the services you provide.
  - It needs to be easy to understand and communicate.
  - It should pay you for what you can control.
- Flat retainers have advantages for both clients and planners.

15 | *Living the Dream*

Don't forget until too late that the business of life is not business, but living.

—B.C. Forbes

"The cobbler's children go barefoot." How often have we heard that metaphor used to describe "experts" who do not apply their expertise for themselves? Doctors who ignore their health, police officers who break the law, lawyers without wills, architects who don't design homes for themselves, insurance agents who are underinsured— the list is almost endless. Of course, there are financial advisers who do not save for the future. More common among financial life planners, however, are those who do not live the lives they encourage their clients to live. The basic theme of financial life planning is that money makes a poor master but a wonderful servant. You can apply that notion to your business or your career. If your business does not serve your life and it *becomes* your life, you may want to ask yourself why you do what you do. Sid Caesar once said, "In between goals is a thing called life, that has to be lived and enjoyed." I would go even further than that. *Enjoying life should be your number one goal.* Building a business and career should not interfere with that goal. In fact, I believe that people who have found balance in their lives build better businesses than those who have made their careers their number one priorities.

Why is it that so many financial planners develop businesses and try to fit their lives into those businesses? The happy financial planners I know focus on building their lives and develop practices that serve those lives. Isn't that what financial life planners counsel their clients to do? I have read and listened to practice development "experts" categorize some financial planning practices as "lifestyle businesses." They differentiate these practices from others that they label as "financially successful." Of course, the implication is obvious: You need to choose between financial success and life success! When we hear that, we wonder if these people have ever interviewed successful planners like Ross Levin, Elissa Buie, Rich and Gayle Colman, Jonathan Guyton, Guy Cumbie, or scores of others who have built very successful practices that serve their lives. Other planners who are becoming slaves to their practices and sacrificing their lives need to follow their examples. We know from our own personal experiences that it is not necessary to sacrifice success in life for business success. In fact, we are convinced that creating a life that is balanced will actually result in a business that is financially rewarding.

Mitch Anthony coined the term "practicide," which he defines as "building a business that will eventually kill you." It has been said that the best gift you can give any client is the example of a life that is working. That is even truer if you purport to offer the promise of financial life planning. After all, what good are you to your clients if you eventually burn out, burn up, or go up in smoke? Therefore, if you are serious about building a financial life planning practice and helping your clients merge their money with their lives, your first step is to do it for yourself. Practice the exercises presented in this book, preferably with another planner who can help you through the process. Enroll in George Kinder's "Seven Stages of Money Maturity" workshop. Consider becoming a member of Mitch Anthony's Financial Life Planning Institute. Take the time to write your answers to the three Kinder questions from Chapter 5. Once you have adopted the principles of financial life planning in your own life, you will be able to help your clients achieve the financial peace of mind they all crave.

I have recounted many stories about clients who are living their dreams, unconstrained by worries they once had about money. That didn't happen because we created money that was not there before we met them. Our process helped them to put it in perspective in relation to what they wanted to accomplish in their lives. They learned that philanthropy, taking their family on a vacation to Europe, buying that second home, changing careers, relocating to buy a farm, reorganizing a business to have more leisure time, and fulfilling other dreams were more important than agonizing over stock market volatility. These people and other clients of financial life planners throughout the country have improved the quality of their lives because of the work we do in our profession. Moreover, the planners I interviewed had as their first priority helping their clients live financially stress-free lives. In addition, while they knew their practices needed to be profitable for them to exist and accomplish their goals of helping clients, making money was not their primary objective. However, they have highly financially successful practices. Is that a paradox? Perhaps, but I have always believed that giving clients what they want and need with integrity is the most profitable business model one can have.

I recently made a life decision that I wanted to live in Florida. You might suppose I could have concluded that I would have to retire from my practice to do so. However, retirement is the last thing that I want to do because I thoroughly enjoy my practice and my interaction with clients. As discussed above, as a financial life planner, I believe that a person's career needs to support his life decisions. Therefore, I have found a way to fit my business into my life. I approached my partners and made the decision to open an office in Fort Myers. I periodically travel to Philadelphia for face-to-face meetings with my clients who live there. The details of the arrangement are not that relevant to the points I am making. What is important is that I am putting my life ahead of my business without sacrificing my business. Mitch Anthony calls it getting a better "return on life."

I have been in financial services for over 40 years. But the last five, since I have been practicing financial life planning, have been the most gratifying as well as the most profitable. There are many doubters in our profession. We are quantitative planners, they tell us. We should not be venturing into nontechnical areas with our clients, they insist. It seems that almost every positive change that has ever occurred in our history has been met with speculation and naysayers. I am reminded of the story about a man and his son, who many years ago, entered a village—the father sitting on his donkey and his son following. Shortly after their entrance, they overheard a vendor say, "Look at that pompous ass, sitting on the donkey like a king, while his poor son walks in the mud." Embarrassed by this, the father climbed off the donkey, hoisted his son onto the donkey and they continued their journey. They turned a corner only to hear another complaint: "Can you imagine the lack of respect that boy shows for his father? He rides and makes his father walk. There was a time when children honored their elders." Concerned by this criticism, the boy and his father both rode the donkey. A passerby yelled, "Animal cruelty! Two people riding on the back of one poor donkey." Not knowing what to do, the father decided that they should both walk beside the donkey. It wasn't very long before they heard someone quip, "Talk about stupidity! Here these people have a beast of burden, yet they walk through the mud." Finally, the father said to the son, "Son, whatever we do, we cannot please everyone. Why don't we just do what we think is right?" I know that it is right to engage my clients in the financial life planning process. I hope that you will too. If you do, I can assure you that you will not only improve the quality of your clients' lives, you will, most assuredly, improve the quality of your life.

Index